AN EDUCATED GUIDE TO
SPEEDING TICKETS
HOW TO BEAT & AVOID THEM!!!

AN EDUCATED GUIDE TO
SPEEDING TICKETS
HOW TO BEAT & AVOID THEM!!!

AUTHORED BY

RICHARD WALLACE II

A Veteran Police Officer Who Shares The
Inside Tips & Strategies With You!!!

PUBLISHED BY
"T-BIRD" BOOKS
A DWIGHT-WALLACE ENTERPRISE
PUBLICATION

210 Park Avenue, Suite234
Worcester, MA 01609
1-888-344-4836
www.dwpubs.com

ACKNOWLEDGEMENTS & DEDICATIONS

The author gratefully acknowledges the invaluable assistance, patience and understanding of his business partner, Richard D. Carrico Jr., and therefore dedicates this book to him for all of his help in putting this project together. "Where does the time go!"

The author would also like to thank Quinn-Woodbine Book Manufacturing for all of their help and assistance, and for their expert and professional advice on making this book a work of art. Thanks!

A special thanks to Rich Swanson for his assistance and advice and whose input was most helpful and appreciated.

TABLE OF CONTENTS

PREFACE AND DISCLAIMER

This Publication is intended to provide guidance in regards to the material covered herein. It is published and sold with the expressed understanding that the Publisher and Author are not herein engaged in providing legal or professional law services, or any other service herein not expressed. If legal or professional advice is required the services of a competent professional should be considered and sought.

This Publication provides an authors opinion in regards to the subject material contained herein. Every effort has been made to make this publication as complete and accurate as humanly possible. This guide should not be used as the ultimate and sole legal source. Laws and procedures change often and therefore, the ultimate source for information are the legal publications in your own state.

Since each case is different, this book is not, nor can it be, a substitute for the services of a competent attorney. An attorney can provide professional advice; consult one when needed.

The Authors and Publishers neither have nor assume liability nor responsibility to any person or entity with respect to any loss or damage caused or alleged to be caused directly or indirectly by the information contained in this Publication. The Authors and Publishers disclaim any personal liability arising out of or incurred as a consequence of the use and application, either direct or indirect, of any advice, information or methods presented herein.

"T-BIRD" BOOKS
A DWIGHT-WALLACE ENTERPRISE PUBLICATION
210 Park Avenue, Suite 234
Worcester, MA 01609
1-888-344-4836

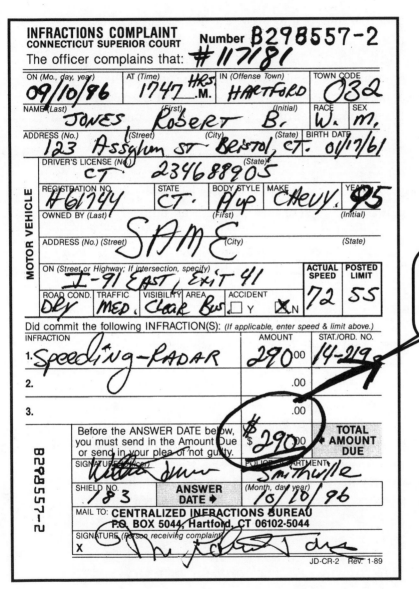

INFRACTIONS COMPLAINT
CONNECTICUT SUPERIOR COURT Number B298557-2

The officer complains that: # 117181

ON (Mo., day, year)	AT (Time)	IN (Offense Town)	TOWN CODE
09/10/96	1747 HRS .M.	HARTFORD	032

NAME (Last)	(First)	(Initial)	RACE	SEX
JONES,	Robert	B.	W.	m.

ADDRESS (No.)	(Street)	(City)	(State)	BIRTH DATE
123	Assylum St	Bristol,	CT.	01/17/61

DRIVER'S LICENSE (No.) CT. 234688905 (State)

MOTOR VEHICLE

REGISTRATION NO.	STATE	BODY STYLE	MAKE	YEAR
H61744	CT.	P/up	CHEVY.	95

OWNED BY (Last)	(First)	(Initial)
SAME		

ADDRESS (No.) (Street)	(City)	(State)

ON (Street or Highway; If intersection, specify)	ACTUAL SPEED	POSTED LIMIT
I-91 EAST, EXIT 41	72	55

ROAD COND.	TRAFFIC	VISIBILITY	AREA	ACCIDENT
DRY	MED.	Clear	Bus	☐ Y ☒ N

Did commit the following INFRACTION(S): (If applicable, enter speed & limit above.)

INFRACTION	AMOUNT	STAT./ORD. NO.
1. Speeding-RADAR	290 00	14-219
2.	.00	
3.	.00	

Before the ANSWER DATE below, you must send in the Amount Due or send in your plea of not guilty.

$ 290 00

TOTAL AMOUNT DUE

SIGNATURE (Officer) POLICE DEPARTMENT Smithville

SHIELD NO.	ANSWER DATE ➤	(Month, day year)
183		10/10/96

MAIL TO: **CENTRALIZED INFRACTIONS BUREAU**
P.O. BOX 5044, Hartford, CT 06102-5044

SIGNATURE (Person receiving complaint)
X

JD-CR-2 Rev. 1-89

B298557-2

Never Pay This Again!

INTRODUCTION AND AUTHORS STORY

If you are right now holding a copy of this book in your hands, you may be among the thousands of drivers and motorists who are stopped and ticketed for speeding each and every day by members of various law enforcement agencies across the country.

If your like many of those thousands of drivers, your mad as hell and would give anything to fight back at the system of which I myself was a part of for many years. I was a police officer in a community in Connecticut for almost 14 years, but because of an injury suffered in the line of duty, I was forced to retire in early 1996. Now because I am about to share with you some of the many inside tips as they pertain to both speeding tickets and speeding itself, you will be able to fight back against speed traps and speeding tickets.

You may have seen some other publications that have been written over the years which provide strategies and tips on beating a speeding ticket in court, and yes, some of the information that was given was helpful, but it was just generally a list of overall guidelines to follow once you got a speeding ticket and then went to court to fight it. All of these tips are very important in the overall picture of you appearing in court to plead or defend your case, but a person needs more than just being told to dress neat or to be polite if they are going to be successful in beating a speeding ticket in court. If that was all there was to beating a speeding ticket, everybody would be pleading not guilty and heading to court to fight those tickets.

This publication differs from those others in many important ways. First, none of the others were written by a former police officer like myself. Who better to know about speeding but a police officer. I will give you those inside tips and strategies best known by the police on how to beat a speeding ticket in court and also how to speed and not get caught! Many of these tips and strategies are generally known to members of law enforcement, but not readily known or used by members of the motoring public, until now that is!

Additionally, I will explain in layman's terms, the types of speed detection devices currently being used by law enforcement today. I will also explain all of their many flaws, which is the most important information you will read in that chapter because it is those flaws that will enable you to beat a ticket in court.

I am sure by now there are many of you who may be asking yourself, *why would a former police officer want to share those secrets about speeding and speeding tickets with the public?* I was a police officer for almost 14 years in Connecticut, and like most people, I had some dreams that I wanted to pursue. I just had enough of the job, found myself getting burned out and just plain sick of seeing everyday average citizens getting stopped by state and local police and ticketed for speeding violations on a daily basis, with most of those tickets being undeserved and unjustified. There is a big difference between a person exceeding the speed limit by 10 - 15 mph, and a person driving 30 mph in excess of the posted speed limit, or in a reckless manner.

In the defense of the hard working members of law enforcement, who perform a thankless job, most are just doing their jobs by following orders from superior officials of their respective agency. This publication is not an attempt to bash members of law enforcement. They do not set the fines for speeding, the legislature does. So as hard as it is, and as much as you may see red when you get a speeding ticket, do not blame the police officer for the total speeding fine given. We all should be blamed for allowing these legislators in every state to set those high speeding ticket fines. Everybody should write to their state legislators and demand the fines for speeding be lowered, and inform them that we are all sick and tired of government trying to balance every town, city or state budget on the backs of the motoring public.

I think we can all agree that speeding fines are too high, and in some states, the fines for speeding top out near $500.00, and then those insurance surcharges we must pay for up to 5 years in some states. And for what? Speeding, that is what! Sometimes the speed being exceeded by a motorist may be only 10 mph over the posted speed limit. Not such a grave crime wouldn't you agree? Yet, that motorist can be expected to pay about $1,000.00 in fines and surcharges for that violation of operating just 10 mph over the posted speed limit.

In short, the entire system of issuing speeding tickets is a money making business for state and local government. It couldn't possibly serve to slow speeders because from my own experience, once a leadfoot, always a leadfoot. And because most drivers do just send in their fines, state or local government and the insurance companies all benefit.

For most people who receive speeding tickets, this is the only law they will ever break in their lives because it is the average law abiding citizen who gets snagged in a speed trap. It is these people who will be forced to suffer up to $1,000.00 expense.

Most people will pay their fines and not fight their ticket in court because of guilt, embarrassment or the fear of losing their fight. I trust that by reading this book, that same person will now go into court confidently, and will be successful in beating that traffic ticket, because I have armed you with the knowledge you will need to WIN!

Friends, speeding does sometime cause accidents and death. I am not writing this book to state that one should be able to speed as fast as they want or where and when they want. On the contrary, speeding in excess where it could be considered dangerous and RECK-

LESS driving, needs to be controlled by law enforcement. For example, one who speeds around hospital or school zones or other congested areas, needs to be stopped and issued a speeding ticket if they are driving reckless in these areas.

My biggest complaint and the problem that I have on the entire speeding ticket issue, is the high fines and years of insurance surcharges that follow. In 1995, many states raised their speeding limits to 65 mph or higher, because our roadways and interstate highways are better designed and constructed and are safe enough for a 65 mph speed limit. Anyone who commutes to work on a regular basis is well aware that on any major roadway or interstate highway, the traffic is moving at 65 mph or higher, and that 65 mph is generally the rule of the road.

The national speed limit of 55 was passed in 1974 to conserve fuel during the fuel crisis that was present in the early 70's. Things have since changed in the last two decades. We no longer have a fuel shortage and no longer have to continue driving 55 mph.

You may feel that raising the speed limits will increase accidents. It might surprise you to know that the Federal Highway Administration and the National Safety Board, found in studies, that motorists traveling 10 - 15 mph faster than the 55 mph posted speed limit, were actually safer drivers with fewer accidents. And further stated that most motorists tend to drive at a speed they feel is safe and reasonable, and will ignore the posted speed limit which they consider to be too low. This is a common sense approach and one that I believe should be followed by every motorist in every state.

Many states have been hesitant to raise their speed limits because of the loss of revenue from speeding tickets. This, coupled with insurance company pressure and lobbyists pressing state government, has resulted in a very long process in many states who have attempted to raise their speed limits. Thankfully, in 1995, President

Clinton signed new legislation allowing each state to set their own speed limits within their own states, without the fear of losing federal aid monies for interstate highway maintenance and construction. Due to this legislation, most states have now raised their speed limits.

Other factors have prompted me to write this book. How many times have you seen an off-duty police officer, either in his cruiser or own personal vehicle, speeding or racing down the highway at incredible speeds, and well in excess of the speed limit. We all have probably seen this at one time or another and are upset over it. We wonder how that officer can stop and ticket others for speeding, when he abuses the speed limit himself, under the protection of his badge while off duty.

We all I am sure, have a horror story about being stopped by a police officer for a speeding violation and were treated like a felon. Many police officers who stop motorists for speeding do, for sure, have serious attitude problems which can upset a law abiding citizen. This of course is certainly not right, and should never ever take place.

Finally, the thing I find most disgusting in this entire speeding matter, is that some law enforcement agencies sole motive for stopping a speeding motorist and issuing a ticket with a heavy fine, is to raise money for their agency itself. These departments earn a cut or percentage of every traffic ticket they issue. That money goes directly back to that police department or agency. In essence, many local police departments nationwide are using our roadways and highways as a sort of fundraiser for the department. Most charities who hold fund raisers have a raffle of some kind, the police, however, will lie in wait for you with a radar gun for you to make a mandatory donation.

What an incentive this can be for a chief of police who needs additional money for a new police cruiser, additional supplies or for anything else. Believe it or not, many cops hit the streets with orders from superiors to issue traffic tickets with the sole purpose of raising revenue for their respective department. Their motive is not law enforcement or safety oriented. This type of motivation can not be considered to be in the best interests of public safety. This I find very unfair, as do most motorists.

It seems as though the entire speeding ticket issue revolves around making money for somebody, be it the local police department, your state, or your insurance companies who reap millions of dollars from insurance surcharges. Would it surprise you to know that in many states, the insurance companies themselves supply the police with those radar and laser guns which enable the police to issue speeding tickets, and thus raising revenue for the insurance companies through the collection of those surcharges. The insurance companies may pay thousands of dollars to supply those police departments with radar and laser equipment, but they make back this money thousands of times over.

As a police officer, I ran radar, made traffic stops, and gave out loads of speeding tickets. I'm guilty, so sue me! But I found it difficult to issue those tickets after a few years because every year the fines would go up and my conscious would bother me. In some states, a fine total can reach $500.00 plus additional court costs. I'd ask myself, if I were to get stopped, could I afford the ticket, and my answer was usually no! Based on that, I generally did not give out tickets worth hundreds of dollars in fines. A written or oral warning in many instances may have been issued instead.

Of course if I stopped a motorist who was operating in a reckless manner or at speeds above 15 mph over the posted limit, I took appropriate action, and rightfully so. The highways need to be patrolled by law enforcement and the nuts need to be ticketed as well as taken off the roadway.

It was during the past few years that I knew that the motoring public needed to be armed with tips and tactics that would enable them to speed without getting caught and to fight a speeding ticket in court and win. I collected my thoughts, wrote them down and felt now was the time to publish this book which you are now holding in your hand.

As you will see, most, if not all of my tips can be used by everybody. The most important tip that I can give you is to always fight a speeding ticket. Your odds of getting at least your fine greatly reduced are very good if you use this book and the information contained herein. Your goal is to have that ticket thrown out of court completely though, and I hope this book will enable you to do just that.

Please understand one thing, this book is ones guide only. It can't take care of everybody's ticket problems, especially if you get stopped for speeding in a reckless manner or at speeds above what I would consider reasonable. Although my strategies and tips may very well work for you, your odds for multiple and repetitive stops for speeding increase dramatically. This book is meant to help the safe and sane driver who travels at speeds higher than the posted speed limit, but does it in a safe and sane manner.

For those of you who might be saying it is a big waste of time to plead not guilty and fight the ticket because that cop has you on a radar backed speeding ticket, I say with confidence, that once you read this book, your opinion will have changed completely. I will leave you with a better understanding of how speed detection devices work as well as their shortcomings. You will be able to challenge and beat tickets in court better than many other people, including police officers and lawyers.

Please remember, this book is only a guide, It should not be taken as legal advice. Every traffic situation is different, and thus carries its own set of circumstances and facts. This book will better serve to educate you and allow you to exercise some options in fighting a traffic ticket from behind the wheel of your car, and before a judge in court. Not everybody will be completely successful in fighting a ticket however, but with this book, the odds are tipped in your favor. You can't win if you don't try. Always remember, regardless of the circumstances of the traffic stop, to FIGHT BACK! It could save you hundreds of dollars in the long run. Good luck and safe motoring.

"Now Roswell, did you remember to engage the radar detector shield? You know if we get to close we'll get picked up on police radar for speeding...Now how would we explain this in court..." "Now don't be crazy! earthlings still deny our existence."

Do you think that radar, laser and vascar can detect the speed of UFOs if they really existed?!

CHAPTER ONE

THE TYPES OF SPEED DETECTION DEVICES BEING USED BY LAW ENFORCEMENT TODAY.

It is in this chapter that I will give you a description of the various speed detection devices that are being used today by members of law enforcement all over the country. I will also include a simplified explanation of how these particular devices operate and how they are used by those enforcement agencies across the nation. Most importantly, I will explain the many shortcomings, and weaknesses each speed detection device has in its application and use.

I believe it is vitally important for all motorists to know something about the various speed detection devices out there being used by law enforcement. By knowing how these devices operate, a person will better understand each device's flaws and weaknesses, and thus will be better prepared should they have to go to court and fight a speeding ticket that they have received.

You need to remember, that each and every speed detection device being used by law enforcement is simply a tool, a piece of equipment, and mechanical in its make up and composition, and thus susceptible to breaking, producing errors, and failing completely.

Each speed detection device being used is only as good as its operator. Nobody is perfect including the equipment itself, all speed detection devices as well as its operators, are prone to flaws, errors and failure. Due to these many reasons, each and every speeding ticket must be fought in a court of law.

Even if you have received a speeding ticket that you felt you deserved, because you were actually speeding, it too has to be fought in court because your goal is to avoid paying any fines or insurance surcharges. Additionally, if you were cited for speeding going with the flow of traffic or on an open roadway where the set speed limit is unreasonable, you may have been the victim of an undeserved speeding ticket and should fight it in court.

RADAR

The first type of speed detection device that is very widely used by law enforcement is, of course, radar. This is the speed detection device we all know and love! But, what really is this thing we call radar anyway?

The word radar is actually an acronym, or abbreviation of the phrase **RA**dio **D**etection **A**nd **R**anging. Radar was first used primarily to detect aircraft and ships that belonged to the enemy in World War II. Shortly after that, traffic engineers utilized radar to determine highway speeds of vehicles.

The early police radar units which were crude bulky units, have evolved into compact highly mobile devices that are being used today. Vast technological advances in the computer industry have been major contributing factors in the development of today's police radar.

Police radar provides a speed reading on a detected target, but not on the range of the target or targets. Thus, police radar can detect the speed of any one of several vehicles traveling at close proximity, and because of that, the law enforcement officer must make the choice himself which vehicle he believes is speeding according to the radar.

For the sake of explanation, and because it is the most widely used radar today, we will discuss modular radar units. That is, two piece units, which include the antenna head and the counting unit. The antenna head sends out the radar beam and receives the reflected radio waves. The counting unit, or box, receives the signal from the antenna, then filters it and converts the signal into miles per hour which then appear in the visual display window. The antenna in the two piece unit, is what is normally observed hanging outside a police cruiser window. The counting unit or box is usually observed sitting on the dashboard of the police cruiser.

Police radar generally operates on one of two principle frequencies or bands, being the "X" and "K" bands. All this really means is a different formula is used for both the "X" and "K" bands for speed measurement and determination. Both are based on a theory called the Doppler Principle.

Christian Doppler, an Austrian physicist is credited with having discovered the fact that relative motion causes a signals frequency to change. He discovered this basic scientific fact by studying sound waves, but it was later found out that the principle applied to all kinds of wave motions including light and radio waves.

Most people have, at one time or another, heard how the Doppler principle affects sound waves. We can explain the Doppler principle in radar terms, as follows:

Whenever there is relative motion between a radar and a solid object, the frequency of the transmitted signal will be different from that of the reflected signal. If the relative motion is bringing the radar and the object closer together, the reflected signal will have a higher frequency than the transmitted signal. If the relative motion is bringing the radar and the object farther apart, the reflected signal will have a lower frequency than the transmitted signal. The speed of the relative motion determines exactly how much higher or lower the reflected signals frequency will be.

What does all this mean? In short, the radar beam frequency will change based on the reflected signal or interference it encounters with a solid object, like an automobile. Due to this interference, the radar signal will change and indicate what the difference of that change is. The radar unit will measure the difference between the outgoing and incoming frequency and then convert that calculation to a miles per hour speed of that object, such as an automobile.

The radar transmitter does not send out energy in all directions. Instead, the antenna head focuses most of its energy into a cone-shaped beam. This radar beam is very similar to the beam of light that is sent out by a searchlight. However, within the cone is a cigar-shaped beam; most of the energy in the radar beam is concentrated into that central core. Within that central core of beam, the concentration or beam strength drops off the further it is from the transmitter. If a target is close to the transmitter, and directly in the path of the greatest intensity of the beam, it will receive and reflect more energy. Thus, the further away an object is from that beam, the less it will receive and reflect energy. This ultimately results in a miles per hour speed reading on the radar control unit.

Hand held police radar units operate in a similar method, except that the antenna and the control unit are all contained within one solid unit, thus, a hand held radar unit. The principle is the same as that of the modular or mobile unit, in that a beam of radar, or a frequency is sent out and reflects off a solid object which then returns that beam to the hand held radar which produces a miles per hour reading of the target. The biggest and most common flaw with police hand held radar, is that many officers will keep the gun down at their side or in their laps in an effort to conceal it. The officer will then raise the gun quickly in order to get the speed of the target vehicle. The problem here lies with the officer raising the radar gun, because the unit will not only now measure your speed, but will **add** the speed of the officers arm in motion. This can **increase** your speed up to 10 mph. Keep your eyes open for hand held radar guns and how and when the officer uses them. This could be very helpful in court and could even be grounds for dismissal.

You should also know that hand held radar guns, or any other type of radar unit emitting nonionizing radiation, can not be used within the confines of a police cruiser in the State of Connecticut. It is actually against the law, under State Statutes of that state because it is believed that the units operated inside a police cruiser increase the risk of the officers getting cancer of some type from the radar radiation.

Now that I have tried to explain, somewhat, how radar itself operates and where the original theory and principle came from, we need to ask "how well does it work, how accurate is it, and can we trust it???"

The use of Police Traffic Radar is so widespread that we naturally assume the technology is reliable. That is unfortunate because Radar makes mistakes. Lots of them.

There have been many unbiased, scientific tests conducted that have shown police radar instruments used in traffic enforcement do work, and are reliable and are effective when carefully installed, properly maintained and operated.

My answer to those questions is that radar **can** work, it **can** be accurate, but it **can't** be trusted to be completely exact in all its applications and uses. There are many types of interferences, flaws, and inaccuracies with police radar. We have all heard about radar clocking trees at 65 mph, houses at 25 mph and high tension wires at 85 mph. Why, and what are the facts about radar and its flaws, problems and weaknesses?

RADAR AND ALL ITS FAULTS

The first, and one of the most significant problems with police radar is like other speed detection devices it is only a mechanical tool, therefore subject to mechanical failure and inaccuracies. Additionally, it is operated by a person and, of course, every human is subject to making mistakes and errors. Manufacturers could design and build the perfect radar unit ever, but, that would not prevent errors based on the expertise of the people whom operate the radar. Does radar itself make mistakes? Or is it the operator whom is making the mistakes?

The answer to that question is both. Radar itself makes mistakes only as far as its inability to detect what is or is not a vehicle that is speeding, (i.e., the speeding house, power line or tree). Radar is a piece of equipment, doing what it is made to do, which is to measure radio and frequency waves of solid objects, regardless of what that object is. The fact is, human error has been the root of almost all successful challenges of radar in court. Remember, radar is only as good as its operator and for a variety of reasons, many of which we will cover as we proceed to discuss the weaknesses and flaws of police radar.

For example, many police radar operators occasionally set up an appreciable distance from the roadway, in order to conduct covert surveillance. Due to this method, the angular effect of the radar signal or beam is magnified meaning that some speeders will escape apprehension because the radar speed measurements are lower than their true speeds. This was mentioned earlier, the closer you are to police radar the more apt your vehicle is to having its speed detected, and the opposite is true if your vehicle is further away from the police radar.

How the police operator aims or points the radar antenna head will greatly impact the magnitude of the angular effect. If radar has been aimed carelessly, the result may be the reading of a speeding vehicle would not be obtained until the vehicle was almost on top of the cruiser. Effectively run radar requires the police officer to properly aim the radar antenna. This keeps the angle factor low and pinpoints vehicles easier.

Not all objects reflect radar energy equally. Metal objects like vehicles, trucks and the like, reflect radar beams very well, as do other objects like stone and concrete. Glass and plastic however, allow most of the radar beam to pass through them with little reflection; just as beams of light pass through. The end result here is, that the amount of energy reflected back from an object depends upon what the object itself is, as well as its size and mass. The radar unit will also read large objects further away from the unit and nonmetallic and smaller objects closer to the unit (such as cars with fiberglass bodies and motorcycles). If you are in an area where the radar beam covers two lanes, and there is another car next to you, radar can not tell the officer who is speeding, according to the radar monitor. Further, if there is a larger and faster moving vehicle such as a truck behind your vehicle, radar will pick up that vehicle speed, but because you are in front, the officer will erroneously believe that you are the speeding vehicle. Be aware for low flying aircraft and trains because of the same reason. If you find yourself being stopped, try to observe if any of these factors apply because they will be very useful when you get to court. This will help to establish a doubt that the radar reading was accurate.

Improper target identification is the most common error that members of law enforcement make everyday. Since radar picks up every moving object the officer must guess or assume who the speeder is, if there is more than one present. An officer who is honest and professional will not ticket somebody unless he is absolutely sure that the reading was caused by a particular vehicle.

Besides operator error, there are many sources of man made interferences. Moving objects, such as rotating signs, because they are moving, reflect a radar beam and will produce a speed reading. This is true also in the movement of fan blades, exhaust fans, air conditioners, and even those from within the police cruiser. This is true because the radar beam is transmitted through the windshield of the patrol car and the cruisers own defroster or air conditioner fan can and do cause ghost readings, that is, a speed reading when there is no target vehicle present. From my own experiences, this is a very common occurrence with police radar.

These types of false readings also occur when other electrical type of devices are in the area, such as a CB or other type of two-way radio. Many officers have CB radios within their cruisers, and therefore, radar interference is a common occurrence. Radio transmitters, and towers are also great sources of radar interference.

Power lines and transformers, neon lights, electrical storms, rain and wind, and other sources of harmonic frequencies can all influence radar readings. I have found from my own experience, that they **all do** quite often. It is because of this interference, police radar should not be operated in the rain or other inclement weather.

Two piece radar units can produce erroneous readings when the police radar operator **"pans"** or **"passes"** the antenna across the display unit inside the cruiser. The antenna passing by the display unit will cause it to give a false reading and will indicate the speed of the police cruiser itself if in fact the car is moving. The cause of this error is electronic feedback between the two units. These units can also give wrong target identification when the **"automatic lock"** feature is being used. This is why the National Highway Traffic Safety Administration has recommended the **"automatic**

lock" feature be disabled. The theory here is that if the unit locks automatically on the speed of an approaching vehicle, the police radar operator may have to "pick" which vehicle may be the actual speeder, and because of that man-made interference, the wrong vehicle could be stopped and ticketed. The NHTSA recommends that police need to provide a **"tracking history"** of that target vehicle, and by the use of the **"auto-lock"**, this is not possible.

Some of radar's other flaws and weaknesses include something called patrol speed **"shadowing"**. This can occur during moving radar operations. Whenever there is slower moving traffic ahead of the police car, there is a good possibility that the radar's low beam component which is supposed to measure the ground or the patrol units speed, will mistake some other object for the ground, and this can result in a lower patrol-speed reading, and produce an equivalent increase in the target speed, thus, giving false readings of oncoming, speeding vehicles.

Another radar flaw is something called **"bumping"**. This can also occur during moving mode radar. Here, the patrol car may begin to brake and slow down, like to reverse direction to proceed after a violator, and what happens is that before the target speed and patrol car speed are locked in, some radar units will **"bump"** the target speed by several miles per hour because it may be including some of the patrol speed. When I operated radar I found this happened quite often.

On the other hand, something called **"batching"** can occur. This happens when the officer quickly accelerates and the radar unit does not immediately adjust for the officers sudden speed, and until it does, it may add that increase of speed of the patrol unit, to the speed of the target- You. This will result in a completely inaccurate reading and probably an undeserved speeding ticket.

One of the more common errors with police radar use, is not actually in the use and application of radar itself. It is in the **"tracking**

history" that errors occur. When two or more vehicles are in radar's range of beam, the operator has to decide which target to select to stop. What should be done by the officer, which is highly recommended in training manuals, but usually is not practiced, is that the officer needs to wait until the vehicles pass by the patrol car. He must then make sure the car being tracked no longer registers a speed reading. This would assure that the correct target vehicle is being tracked and subsequently stopped. This is one of "Instant Radar's" problems because it does not provide that traffic history. What the officer should be doing in developing that traffic history is having the radar on prior to stopping vehicles for speeding. The officer should be in the process of determining if there are any interference signals in the area, like from a CB or other type of radio, power lines and other electronic magnetic interference. Since there is **NO** real standard to beam width of radar, it is impossible to determine how wide a range of targets the unit might be covering at the time of the reading of vehicles in that area. This is why the officer has to observe a vehicle he believes to be speeding and "track" the area, as well as the traffic. The officer needs to track the speed as indicated on radar, to make certain that the speed indicated is accurate. This may mean observing the speed of the vehicle change several times. In my own experiences, I would always check a vehicle speed by observing the control unit showing the speed of the target vehicle and watch for the changes so that an accurate tracking history took place. Since this is not done by many law enforcement officers, it may be one of the reasons there are so many bad arrests and convictions for tickets issued based on police radar because of that operator error.

As mentioned previous, police moving radar is full of flaws and weaknesses, and in many state courts, moving radar issued tickets are not prosecuted and are usually dismissed. Moving radar will always produce spurious or ghost readings as a police cruiser travels upon a roadway. These readings can be caused by reflections of the beam from stationary objects along the roadway like billboards, overpasses, high tension wires and the like. You need to be observant for these types of objects should you get stopped for speeding by a member of law enforcement.

PHASE-LOCK LOOP (PLL) RADAR

To further complicate the entire traffic radar problem, modern traffic radar has changed some and no longer relies on direct measurement of frequency changes to determine target speed. Instead, new circuitry known as Phase-Lock-Loop or (PLL) radar is used, which interprets the microwave shift and displays it as a digital readout in miles per hour. The advantages are that its small, costs less and can more easily read its targets. The disadvantages are an excessive range, up to a mile and a half for some models, and a tendency to lock on the first good target, and stay there tracking it. This new unit can also produce something called **"harmonic error"** which could cause a doubling or tripling of the speed of the target vehicle should it be traveling at 20 mph or less. This occurs for example, when a patrol car is slowing down or changing speed and a target vehicle is accelerating from a slow speed. If the officer is not observing traffic carefully, or has obtained the reading from a distance, an unjustified speeding ticket may be issued.

In closing this chapter on police radar, I want to mention a few things about one radar unit currently used in many states, including Alabama, California, Delaware, Florida, Illinois, Louisiana, Maine, and New York. This radar Unit is called *Stalker* and is manufactured by Applied Concepts of Plano, Texas. What is unique about this radar speed detection unit, is that it operates on a KA wide band frequency, with a 6,000 foot range, and has the ability to track the speeds of vehicles both in front of and behind the cruiser. These units will work in the moving mode with the cruiser operating as slow as 1 mph, whereas other types of moving radar require the cruiser to be operating about 20 mph.

These Stalker units are very expensive, and are very good radar speed detection units. Their radar beams however, can be detected by most radar detectors on the market now, that already detect normal X and K Band radar as well as laser. Using the same strategies, tips and tactics as already explained about other types of police radar, Stalker based speeding tickets can be challenged in court the same way.

Notwithstanding all of the information we have just presented, current models of police radar can and do accurately measure speed of vehicles, provided, the road is straight, visibility is good, traffic is light, and the officer has been properly trained in radar use, and is able to ignore all spurious signals. Of course, these ideal conditions do not often exist, so therefore, there will be errors, which can be challenged in court.

As you can see, police radar itself, is indeed **not** perfect, **not** fool proof or **100%** accurate. And if properly challenged in a court of law, can be defeated. It is important to remember courts not only want to know the scientific accuracy and reliability of a particular speed detection device, it wants to establish the qualifications of the officer using it. Radar itself must be accurate, and needs to be tested.

OPERATOR QUALIFICATIONS

Many courts have little difficulty in outlining the qualifications it deems acceptable for police radar operators. Most have said that it is sufficient to qualify an operator provided he has the knowledge and training that enables him to properly set up, test and read the radar instrument. It is not, however, necessary for the officer to know or understand the scientific principles or be able to describe the inner workings of a radar unit. A few hours of instruction and hands on use is normally enough to qualify an operator. Many states require the officer to receive some type of radar certification which is documented within department records should that officer need to appear in court on a radar issued traffic ticket. Most officers nationwide, have in fact received this type of training.

The National Highway Traffic Safety Administration in a publication entitled "Police Traffic Radar", in February 1980, (reference number DOT HS-805 254), which many departments nationwide have adopted as their standards, calls for a minimum of 24 hours of classroom and 16 hours of supervised field experience for the use and training of police radar. Further, the NHTSA calls for retraining every one to three years. Something most officers do not receive after their initial training within their respective law enforcement agency. This is one area that we will discuss later because that failure to retrain could result in your ticket being dismissed in court.

RADAR ACCURACY

The courts cannot simply accept every single radar speed detection device to be totally accurate at all times. Proof must be supplied to demonstrate that a particular device was functioning properly at the time that it was used to obtain a speed reading of the target vehicle. In doing so, the courts can reasonably assume that if a particular device was checked for accuracy at various times, through accepted methods, then readings obtained could be perceived to be accurate and acceptable.

The most efficient, convenient and accurate method for testing or calibrating the accuracy of any given radar unit, is through the use of a tuning fork. The use of tuning forks was established as an accurate method by the Supreme Court of the State of Connecticut in **STATE VS. TOMMANELLI,** in 1966. However, the accuracy of the tuning fork may be challenged by the defendant. If no challenge is offered, the accuracy of the tuning fork will stand as well as the accuracy of any device which was properly tested by that tuning fork.

Tuning fork calibration works like this; when struck against an object, it emits a humming sound and then that tuning fork is then held near the antenna of the radar unit and a reading will show up on the control unit. Each tuning fork is designed to emit a frequency that corresponds to a particular mph and when held near the antenna, that frequency should be the reading shown. If it does, the unit is probably accurate and working properly. If it does not, the radar unit may be defective and therefore, very inaccurate, and should not be used.

The National Bureau of Standards and the National Institute of Science and Technology both recommend that police radar be calibrated twice yearly, along with the tuning forks for each respective police radar unit. The problem with this is that these are only recommendations. The lack of generally accepted standards for equipment performance, training requirements or enforcement policies undoubtedly contributes to the misuses and abuses of police radar.

VIOLATOR IDENTIFICATION

In addition to the establishment of the speed of the vehicle, the officer using radar must be able to prove that a particular speed law was violated. The officer must also identify the driver responsible, and that the offense occurred on a public way. In cases where radar was used to obtain a speed measurement, the officer must also be able to identify the violator's vehicle and how he made the determination that the vehicle in question was in fact the violator's, whose speed measurement was obtained. This brings us back to the **"tracking"** of a vehicle that was discussed earlier.

Courts have outlined that an officer should estimate the speed of the target or suspected vehicle through visual observations. Once that vehicle has been singled out, if that theory is possible, then the radar can be used to confirm the speed. That is provided, however, that the target vehicle was **out front, by itself**, when the speed reading took place and that it was the **closest** vehicle to the radar at the time of the alleged violation. All of this of course, is something that you will need to remember if and when you are stopped. This information is important when you go to court to fight that speeding ticket. See page #31 for an example of improper target ID.

CASE PREPARATION & PRESENTATION FOR COURT

When presenting a case for court, an officer will need to prepare himself. He must be able to establish and keep these elements in mind:

a. The officer must be able to establish the time, place, and location of the radar device, the location of the offending vehicle, the clocked speed, and the posted speed limit in that area at the time of the violation.

b. The officer must state and present his qualifications and certifications on radar use.

c. He must provide the actual radar unit used or at least indicate the manufacturer and model name.

d. He must establish that the speed detection device was operating properly. He must also provide the units calibration and maintenance records, as well as any tuning forks used with that radar device.

e. The officer should identify the vehicle and indicate how and when he made the visual estimate of the violation, thus provide a **"tracking history"** of that vehicle.

f. He must include in that **"tracking history"** that the violator vehicle was out front, by itself, when the speed reading was taken.

g. If moving radar was used, the officer must testify that the patrol speed was verified by the comparison of the readout against the cruiser's speedometer, and that the patrol speed was steady. Of course, cruiser speedometer calibrations must be given in this instance also.

h. The officer should provide his agency's FCC (Federal Communications Commission) license, which is required by law. Every law enforcement agency that uses radar must have a license from the FCC to do so. If it doesn't, not only is your ticket dismissed, but that police agency could be in serious trouble.

i. Additionally, some states, (Connecticut being one of them) require the operator to show that radar was being operated in an area with minimum distortion.

j. Finally, some states require that the radar or other speed detection device was expertly tested within a reasonable time following the arrest by means other than internal calibration of that particular unit. This includes laser, which at this time, only has internal calibration as a means to calibrate itself.

Much of the information that I have presented to you so far, is very important. It is in fact this information that will enable you to challenge a speeding ticket in court for a variety of different reasons, many of them proving to be very solid and defensive tactics, as you challenge your speed detection device based speeding ticket.

NHTSA RADAR TEST RESULTS

Police traffic radar was coming under close scrutiny in the late 70's and early 80's, the National Bureau of Standards, under contract from the National Highway Traffic Safety Administration, conducted tests on six different police radar units, and the result of those tests, were surprising.

The public learned from that study that radar does make mistakes, has flaws, and could be challenged in a court of law. The tests revealed quirks in circuitry and in other units, showed **"beam width"**, **"auto-lock"**, **"panning"**, **"shadowing error"**, and **"batching error"** problems. All of these principles have already been discussed. The public learned that no standards existed for the beam width of police radar, which meant the operator had no way of knowing how wide of a range his radar beam might cover. Due to this problem, he would have no idea which target or vehicle would be the actual speeder as indicated on the radar unit. What those radar unit tests showed was that the radar devices were far from reliable.

In addition to these test results, the National Highway Traffic Safety Administration and several other major research institutions have concluded that in fact, police traffic radar itself has little or no effect on speed behavior or accidents. Radar's usefulness is in making arrests easier and quicker. A law enforcement officer can certainly write far more tickets with radar than without it.

The studies show that if used effectively, radar can be used to promote effective traffic enforcement. A visible patrol car itself can act as a deterrent to hostile and aggressive driving. In most cases, police radar is not used in the dangerous or difficult areas of a highway where speeding tends to be a problem. Rather, it is most often used where driving conditions are the safest, like on a well maintained multiple lane highway, and where the traffic is usually operating in excess of an unreasonably low speed limit.

Another study undertaken in 1985 by the International Association of Chiefs of Police, detailed a report on 24 models of the latest types of police radar. The final results of that study showed over 200 individual test failures for police radar, which included everything from errors in tuning fork calibration, to extra sensitive readings caused by electromagnetic interference. In short, their study also showed that police radar was again, unreliable.

Sadly, even with these test results that show the problems with police radar, very little has changed over the years in an attempt to correct the problem. People should have been enraged and demanded repeal of the speeding laws that allowed radar to be used by the police, who themselves, were inadequately trained to operate the units in the first place. Insurance companies should have stopped charging surcharges on its policies because somebody received a speeding ticket. None of these things have happened. Probably because people refused to believe that police radar was unreliable. Another reason may be that the states and insurance companies feared losing too much money, and so they both fought all efforts to make any much needed changes in this area.

LASER- (LIDAR)

A second speed detection device that is becoming more and more popular with law enforcement, is called laser. Laser is also referred to as "lidar" or **LI**ght **D**etection **A**nd **R**anging. By now, I am sure many of you have heard of laser, as the latest speed detection device being used by members of law enforcement in speed control. I am sure though, many of you do not know very much about it.

Laser speed detection equipment sends out a very thin or straight line type of beam, unlike radar's beam which starts out thin and funnels out like the beam of a flashlight. This beam of thin invisible infrared light is projected in a series of about 40 very short energy pulses per second, which move in a straight line, reflecting off a vehicle and returning to the laser gun. Laser uses these light pulses to measure the distance to a vehicle. Speed is then calculated by measuring how quickly these pulses are reflected given the known speed of light. Laser, because of its thin beam, is far more accurate in determining a target vehicles speed. And laser units can be used either day or night. This is all bad news for the motorist, but there is some good news about laser or lidar.

Laser beams are limited to line of sight, meaning the law enforcement officer using laser equipment has to **"see"** your vehicle before he can use the laser gun, and he then has to physically aim the laser gun toward your vehicle. The laser beam is generally aimed directly at the front license plate because it provides a flat, reflective surface and thus a very accurate speed reading for the officer. In short, the officer has to be an expert marksman because he is actually aiming and focusing the laser beam on your vehicle as it approaches. So the key here is if you spot a police cruiser on the side of the road, or any suspicious vehicle parked there, slow down. It could be a police officer using a laser speed detection device, and he could have it pointed right at you. Additionally, laser can only be operated in the stationary mode, and not in a moving vehicle.

Laser, because of that limited line of sight, can not work, and will not work around corners. Again, the officer using the laser, has to "see" your vehicle first before he can use the laser gun. Like radar, if you have two vehicles close by, it is possible that the officer is aiming at you, but getting a reading off the car next to you. Since the beam is invisible, the officer does not know this. But now you do.

Another downside to the use of laser guns is that they generally only have a quarter mile range to them. Again, a police cruiser sitting one mile ahead, under normal circumstances, operating laser, should not be able to detect a speed of an approaching vehicle. This brings me to my theory again, to slow down immediately if any vehicle is observed parked on either side of the roadway ahead. It could very well be a police officer, because many law enforcement agencies use many different vehicle types when operating speed detection devices.

Other more common errors with laser include something called refraction and reflection. With refraction, the laser beam can be bent or refracted differently based on the temperature of air the beam strikes. This is because light is refracted differently by hot air, than by cooler air, and if the beam strikes one or the other, it can confuse the laser unit. In reflection, the laser beam does just that, it reflects off more than one solid object before returning to the unit itself, resulting in a fouled speed calculation.

Some other interesting tips about laser is that because they require more skill to use than normal police radar, they are not all that popular with members of law enforcement. They are big bulky units, they actually look like a video camcorder, they are very expensive also. Another reason is that laser is new, and not all that widespread in use at the present time. The insurance companies are trying hard to change that because they are now in the process of giving laser units to various law enforcement agencies nationwide. Why? Because the more speeding tickets law enforcement issue, the more money insurance companies can charge in surcharges.

Laser, like radar speed detection devices, can not or should not be used in foul or inclement weather like rain, snow or fog. It also can not be used through glass like radar. The laser gun has to be pointed or aimed outside the police cruiser or through an open window. If it is used through glass, the range of the beam is greatly reduced.

Laser uses light to measure speed. It has been shown that the darker your vehicle is, the harder it is for laser to pick up a speed reading from that vehicle. For instance, a black vehicle may absorb all of the light of the laser beam, thus there will be no speed reading indicated on the laser gun. Laser has to reflect off something on a vehicle in order for the complete speed calculation process to take place. A vehicle with little or no chrome makes it hard for laser to get a reading. As do colors that do not reflect light as easily, like black, blue or brown, instead of brighter colors, like red, white or yellow. As well, the more aerodynamic the vehicle is, the more it will deflect the radar beam and give an inaccurate reading.

Using headlight covers and vehicle bras greatly reduce your chances of a laser beam picking up your vehicle and giving a speed reading. The key here is to deflect the laser beam light, not reflect it. Larger vehicles like trucks and vans are easily picked up by laser because of their size and makeup. Some people also believe having very powerful driving lights can throw off the laser beam signal. In bright daylight, aiming laser at or toward the sun can destroy the laser diode or beam.

Equally as effective is the removal of the front license plate or the purchase of a laser cross-section reducing license plate cover. Your goal is to reduce the range and return factor of the laser beam.

Just as there are radar detectors being manufactured to warn motorists about a radar speed detection device further ahead, there are now laser detectors also. I would strongly recommend a person who is in the habit of exceeding the speed limit, purchase a superior quality detector which incorporates both the radar and laser detection capabilities.

Being that laser is relatively new, it has yet to become readily accepted by the court systems as foolproof and 100% accurate. One reason for that is because laser, unlike a radar unit, can not be calibrated externally before or after each motor vehicle stop, like police radar units can.

The State of New Jersey, because of a recent court decision by the Honorable Superior Court Judge Reginald Stanton, on June 13th, 1996, can no longer use laser or lidar gun as evidence to prosecute pending or future speeding tickets. Judge Stanton ruled that he was not convinced that laser readings are accurate or reliable. Due to that ruling, thousands of speeding tickets that had been issued based on laser, were thrown out of court. Judge Stanton pointed out in his ruling that there is no independent test data generated thus far, to back up lasers claim to be accurate within one mile per hour, plus or minus. What further prompted this judge to issue such a decision was that the defense in the trial pointed a laser gun at a wall in the court and got a reading of 4 mph. This court judge decision will undoubtedly have ramifications throughout the nation because other states will begin to use this ruling, or at least examine it worthiness.

In the state of Vermont, laser is currently also undergoing challenges in court. Defense experts there are attempting to show that laser is accurate for measuring distance, but the technology used is not always accurate for calculating speed. The defense experts claim that the crystal based mechanism in the laser is unstable in the nanoseconds between pulses, and the results could be errors of 5 mph or more in speed readings. The manufacturer in this case, Kustom Electronics, claims the error to be plus or minus 1 mph, and that their laser unit is accurate and reliable.

Laser, by manufacturer specifications, should have three basic tests prior to use. The first is the alignment test, which is done to be sure the laser beam is right on its targets and therefore, accurate. The second test is a precision distance test, which is a test just like its name says, that will check the distance between a target and the unit to be sure it is accurate and true. The final test is one called the internal self test. Here the laser unit will check itself internally, and most of its components to be sure all are working properly. If the unit detects an internal problem, it will shut itself off and will not work. The problem with the self test is that it only partially checks the laser device. What the self test does not test are the units analog circuitry, namely, the infrared transmitter and the infrared receiver sections. Subject to this, laser testing itself, has limited value and worth.

There has yet to be an actual speed measurement testing device, such as a tuning fork, that can actually check the laser for reliability and accuracy. Based on this, questions are raised about the validity of laser itself as a source of speed detection and measurement.

Some states, Connecticut included, require that any speed detection device, including laser, vascar or radar, be expertly tested. The testing should be performed within a reasonable time following an arrest by means other than an internal calibration of the equipment itself. For radar, of course, tuning forks are the instrument used to expertly calibrate the unit, but as mentioned before, no such external method exists for laser as of yet. At this time, laser based tickets are being dismissed and or reduced in the State of Connecticut because of this loophole in the law. So be sure you are aware of your own state's law concerning the requirements pertaining to equipment calibration.

As you can see, as effective as laser detection can be, it can also be just as ineffective under the right set of circumstances and conditions. It is at those times you want to always be aware, should you get stopped for speeding and the ticket is issued based on a laser speed detection device.

In preparation for a good solid defense in court against that laser based speeding ticket, one will need to remember a few things. First, has laser been accepted in your state as reliable and accurate? If you do not know, find out. Laser could very well be under judicial challenge in your own state right now. Further, does the laser measurement guarantee that its readings are accurate and reliable 100%, to the extent that nobody will receive a speeding ticket unfairly? If the state calls an expert witness from a laser manufacturer to testify in court on behalf of laser, you need to ask that person if they have a financial interest in seeing that the courts uphold this laser device as accurate and reliable. Further push the issue by adding that the future job status of that employee depends, in part, on the outcome of the many challenges currently ongoing nationwide against the speed detection devices.

VASCAR

The next speed detection device that I will discuss is a device called Vascar, which again, is not all that widely used by members of law enforcement nationwide. This is due to the large expense of the equipment as compared to that of conventional radar equipment. Vascar stands for **V**isual **A**verage **S**peed **C**omputer **A**nd **R**ecorder. In its use and application, it works like this.

The law enforcement officer using Vascar will drive over a specified distance on a highway and will record how long it took, time wise, to cover that distance in his patrol unit. This information is then entered into the computer within the vascar unit operated by the law enforcement officer. When a vehicle enters and leaves that measured area, the computer will give a speed reading. It will then indicate how long or fast, time wise it took for that target vehicle to travel that measured distance. It will also give the speed the vehicle traveled to achieve that time of travel. For example, if it actually took 60 seconds to travel one mile, then we know a vehicle was traveling at 60 mph. On the other hand, if it took 30 seconds for a vehicle to travel that same mile, we then know that the vehicle was traveling at 120 mph, in that same one mile stretch of distance.

Vascar is widely used by aircraft above a highway, with that aircraft measuring the time it took a vehicle to travel from one certain point on a roadway, to another spot or location on the same road. You may have noticed many painted white lines or markings on major highways that seem to be exact in their distance apart from each other. In these areas, law enforcement is most likely using Vascar speed detection devices. When using VASCAR, the aircraft will radio the speed and description of the target vehicle to patrol cruisers below and then a stop will be made and a speeding ticket issued. This is of course, a practice that is full of problems especially for proper vehicle identification. The officer on the ground is relying solely on the description of the target vehicle as given by the officer in the aircraft. It is important to point out that improper identification can and does occur. Additionally, if you are issued a ticket under these circumstances, both of the law enforcement officers need to appear in court to testify. Many times law enforcement officers do not want to waste their time by having to go to court.

There has not been a detector manufactured yet that can detect vascar being in use. Vascar is a very accurate method of determining speed as long as the law enforcement officer using it is honest in his calculations and in the proper selection of reference points.

Be cautious, for that police cruiser that goes speeding by you on a highway. That officer could pass by and at the same moment start measuring your distance and time, and as he speeds off into the sunset, as you proceed up over a hill or around a corner, there he is, waving you over. He has determined that your speed was excessive based on the time it took you to travel the distance he has set on the Vascar unit. In some states, this is considered a speed trap and could be illegal.

Vascar's week points include the fact that the operators reaction time in starting and stopping the device can be large enough to distort speed readings by 15 to 20%. Vascar evidence may be unreliable if the reference points themselves, were unsuitable, if the target vehicle was not clearly identified, or if the distance between the reference points were measured inaccurately. One should be aware of these weaknesses, should they receive a vascar backed speeding ticket.

PACING

Pacing is a method where an officer will try to match the speed of your vehicle with his vehicle and then stay with you for as long as he feels necessary. Pacing is also sometimes called "clocking". The longer the pace the more accurate it will be. The officer will note the speed of his cruiser speedometer and then stop you. There is no requirement as to the length of the pace prior to being stopped.

In these cases, it is important to determine how the officer made the pace. For example, did he speed up to catch your vehicle, and then make the stop? A good driving tip for this type of speed enforcement is to always be aware of who is around you and your vehicle. Watch the road at all times for the police.

The best possible attack on a pacing issued speeding ticket is to ask the officer or his law enforcement agency for that cruiser speedometer calibration records. Try to obtain these records before going to court. Look for any inaccuracies, discrepancies or unusually high maintenance records for that cruiser. Most states and law enforcement agencies require their fleet of police cruisers to have annual speedometer certifications. However, there are many busy agencies who do not have the time to perform calibrations on each and every cruiser. If you are able to show that it has been a while since that cruiser (which was used to issue you a speeding ticket) had been calibrated, you may have just succeeded in raising doubt about the accuracy of that speeding ticket, and you may have it dismissed in court.

You need to remember this as well; if an officer of some law enforcement agency observes your vehicle traveling at what he believes is a high rate of speed, based on his training and experience, and he is not operating any type of speed detection device, nor could he get an accurate pace or clock on you, he could very well stop you for that speeding violation, but he can do very little, enforcement wise. This is because the courts have generally held that without evidence from either radar, laser or some other speed detection device, there is no way for that officer to accurately know your vehicles speed. Due to this, the courts generally dismiss this type of speeding ticket.

Don't think that law enforcement officer is doing you a favor when he stops you for speeding, lectures you, and then does not issue a speeding ticket. It could be that he knows he has no evidence to back up his initial observations of your alleged speed, and also realizes that all he can do is lecture you.

Don't be afraid to ask the officer who stops you what type of speed detection device he was using at the time you were stopped. He could very well be using his personal observations and may now realize that you know he should not issue a speeding ticket to you because he did not clock or pace your vehicle, nor was he using a speed detection device, other than his eyes to get a speed reading from your vehicle. Should you receive a speeding ticket under these circumstances, you have a great chance for dismissal of that ticket in court. So fight it!

Be wary though, pacing can be performed by a cruiser in back as well as in front of your vehicle. Don't assume a police cruiser in front is not pacing your vehicle as he travels down the highway. You do not want to be surprised by getting stopped by that officer who just passed you because you did not know that he could pace your vehicle while traveling in front.

PHOTO OR CAMERA RADAR

The final detection device that I will discuss, is something that has only just begun to be used here in the United States, and that is something called photo or camera radar. It is very widely used in European countries as a means of issuing speeding tickets.

Photo or camera radar, works exactly like it sounds. A camera is attached to a radar unit, along with a computer. The computer is programmed to tell the camera when to take a photo of any vehicle observed exceeding a certain speed limit. Some cameras will take a photo of the front and rear of the vehicle, in an attempt to show the face of the operator as well as the registration number of the target vehicle. Some foreign countries hold the vehicle registration owner liable for the speeding ticket even if they were not the operator at the time of the violation.

What happens next, is that the photos with legible license plates are sorted out, the registration numbers are run into the motor vehicle computer and tickets are then mailed out to the corresponding registered owners.

A successful challenge to a photo radar ticket is achieved by looking at three important things. Statistics have shown that the vast majority of these photo radar tickets are illegible because of these reasons:

1. Illegible license plate number.
2. Make and model of the car is or is not identifiable.
3. Indistinguishable driver or operator.

If you have received such a photo or camera ticket, immediately appeal it and ask to see the photo records that supported a ticket being mailed to you. Look to see if any of those reasons apply and then explain it to the court official hearing your appeal case.

Remember, radar itself has flaws, so ask to look at the records of the piece of equipment that contained the radar unit. Be sure it has been calibrated, were tuning forks used, etc. Refer back to the information that I have provided about radar itself in this chapter. Camera radar can produce false speed readings for sure. It can result in erroneous target identification when more than one vehicle is present in the photo or area. These tickets should always be challenged in court.

A word of caution however, in some other countries, you may be guilty regardless of who, what, where, how, or why. That is just the way some foreign countries work. Be careful if you decide to challenge a speeding ticket in another country.

Some helpful tips to make your vehicle less noticeable or detectable to a photo radar station, is to keep the license plate somewhat dirty. Or try taking off the front license plate so that the front camera can not record the plate number. Be careful though, because in some states you can get a traffic ticket for not having the front plate on your vehicle. Some motorists have painted their plates in a high gloss clear coat paint to make the photos glossy and thus, making the license plate illegible. Generally speaking, anything that can distort your vehicle registration number plate, could work if you frequently travel through an area where photo or camera radar is used.

RADAR DETECTORS - FRIEND OR FOE?

In closing out this chapter, I feel the need to discuss briefly, the radar detector. For the sake of clarification, a radar detector, when used or stated as such, may or may not include the ability to detect laser (lidar) speed detection devices. This is because there are many detectors sold today that detect only radar, and there are equally as many that detect both radar and laser.

There are just as many proponents as there are opponents of radar detectors, and for a variety of different reasons. Some special interest groups claim that radar detectors cause speeding and accidents. As mentioned earlier in this chapter, there is no evidence to date that radar detectors cause higher speeds or play a significant role in causing widespread accidents.

Average traffic speeds are determined by the public's own view of what they perceive to be safe and reasonable at the time. Radar detector owners are generally safe drivers. Some surveys have shown that drivers whom used detectors had fewer accidents per mile than non-owners and drove more miles between accidents also and more often wear their safety belts.

This does not say that there are not people who possess detectors who drive like hostile and dangerous drivers. This is of course true. Some of these drivers undoubtedly believe that by having a detector they are immune from being stopped and ticketed, until it happens. It is then they realize they are just as susceptible to being caught for speeding as somebody who does not have a detector. Such gross driving habits will come to the attention of law enforcement with or without police radar being in use.

Banning radar detectors will not make the "unsafe" driver become a "safe" driver. Only education and sound enforcement programs will accomplish that.

Nonetheless, every year, insurance lobbyists in many states try to pass legislation that will ban the radar detector. More than 100 attempts to ban radar have taken place in different states over the years, and all have been defeated. Only the states of Virginia and the District of Columbia now ban radar detectors. All states however, have bans on detectors for operators of commercial vehicles, like tractor trailer operators. This is a ban I agree with however, because tractor trailer rigs should not be speeding down the highway. These types of vehicles do not stop like a passenger vehicle, and therefore, should not be speeding. Tractor trailer trucks weigh several tons and have far greater destructive capabilities if driven recklessly.

Today insurance company lobbyists actively promote such goals as mandatory insurance coverage and increased use of surcharges, which only better themselves, not their clients. It is the insurance companies who are speaking out in favor of bans on radar detectors, saying that they encourage speeding. Again, studies have shown nothing of the kind, yet, the media takes this misrepresentation and reports on it, and starts calling for bans on radar detectors.

Additional opposition to radar detectors come from law enforcement itself. Many officers do not like detectors because it "challenges" their ability to do their job and makes it more difficult to stop motorists and write them tickets.

The final group of people whom oppose radar detectors, are the public officials who are under pressure from the first two groups: law enforcement and the insurance industry, to make roads safe for all. The approach the public officials take is to blame the radar detector.

Again, traffic experts and many studies have shown the facts to be a little clearer. Radar alone has no influence on traffic speeds or accidents. They know most people drive a safe and reasonable speed, even if it exceeds the posted speed limit. And that by merely possessing a radar detector, one does not automatically become a speeding or reckless driver, or one who increases the risk for an accident, and thus, becomes a maniac on the highways.

Speeding tickets are a basis for money making for the state, city or town, and the insurance companies. The Insurance Institute for Highway Safety (IIHS), a multi-million dollar tax exempt agency, uses its resources to promote unrealistically low speed limits, combined with covert methods of enforcement, only for the sake of lining its own pockets.

What does all of this mean? It means that you as a motorist have the right to own and possess a radar detector. Everybody should consider purchasing a superior quality radar and laser detector, It will greatly help you avoid a much undeserved speeding ticket. I strongly advocate the purchase of such detectors.

As a footnote to page # 15, concerning radar tracking problems, one such example of radar's target tracking that results in an error in target identification, can be the following. A patrol car operating radar is sitting over the crest of a hill. The officer can NOT observe traffic until a vehicle comes over the hill, and he will be watching through his mirrors. The radar unit, however, will pick up and indicate the speed of a vehicle approaching the hill and cruiser BEFORE the vehicle is visually observed by the officer. So, for example, the radar equipment indicated to the officer that a vehicle is approaching at say 75 mph in a 55 mph zone, this will be indicated on the radar control unit, but the officer does not yet observe the vehicle in his mirrors, many times, the officer assumes the first vehicle over the crest of the hill is the car that is speeding. Remember, radar does NOT identify the car that is speeding, the officer does So as you can see, there is clearly room for many errors here. Radar picks up the fastest and largest moving objects first, and it may not necessarily be the first vehicle that comes over the hill that is the actual speeder.

"Oh no...Remember don't panic, stay calm, be polite, both hands on the wheel, make eye contact, here he comes... OOPs the batteries for the mini recorder aren't working..."

If all else fails...pray to the heavens!

CHAPTER TWO

THE MOTOR VEHICLE STOP- "IT ALL BEGINS HERE!"

Nobody likes getting stopped by a member of law enforcement for a traffic violation. Most people, even cops themselves, get nervous when they see those red and blue lights in their rear view mirror. This is not the time to get nervous however, it is a time to remain calm and think clearly. Everything you do from this point on, can either make, or break your case should you receive a speeding or traffic ticket.

Before I begin to explain what needs to be done at the scene of any traffic stop, I am going to suggest that every person operating upon the highways make a purchase of a small mini-cassette recorder, and carry it inside their vehicle at all times. Everything that is said by both that law enforcement officer and you is crucial to your case. As I explain why the motor vehicle stop can make or break your case in court, you will better understand why a mini-cassette recorder is so important.

Once you realize that you are being stopped or pulled over for a traffic offense by a member of law enforcement, there are some commonly known things that you as a motorist must do. The first of course, is to remain calm and begin to pull your vehicle over to the side of the roadway. Do this with caution and care. Pull well enough off the roadway so that the officer is not standing in the middle of the roadway when he approaches and stands outside of your vehicle. It is also a wise idea to put on the vehicle hazard lights, and stay inside your vehicle until the officer approaches you. Never get out and walk toward the officer or his cruiser. This could be taken as an act of aggression by the officer and you may find yourself in much deeper trouble than being stopped for a traffic violation.

From my own experience, a traffic stop was one of the most dangerous and risky duties for a police officer. You just never know who you may be stopping for a minor traffic violation. Due to this, many officers use a lot of caution when making traffic stops. It is your obligation to cooperate with that officer and show him that you are not a threat to him in any way.

If you have taken my advice and purchased a mini-cassette recorder, now is the time to turn it on and conceal it someplace on or near the drivers door so that it can record all conversations that take place on this traffic stop. It would be helpful to have the vehicle registration and your license ready. You should keep your hands in plain view or both resting on the top of the steering wheel. Turn off your radio if it is on. If you are wearing sunglasses, take them off and look the officer in the eyes, this makes things a little more personable, if such a thing can take place. If you are smoking, put it out. You need to get the officer to feel he is safe around you and your vehicle. Do not make any sudden or quick movements because this may be taken as a sign of hostility by the officer. You do not want to upset him in any way.

One word of advice though, if you have a radar detector, leave it where it is. The officer probably already saw it and an attempt to hide it could make him upset because you are now trying to hide something.

Once he feels safe and is comfortable in this traffic stop, the officer will approach your vehicle and ask to see your vehicle registration and license. He may then inform you why you and your vehicle were stopped. Listen to him, do not volunteer any information such as *"everybody else was going the same speed"*, or *"I knew I was speeding but did not know it was that fast."* Remember, the officer will record everything you say on paper and you should be recording everything that is said on your mini-cassette recorder. It is important that you do not say or do anything to incriminate yourself. Continue to remain calm and cooperative at all times. Look at the officer in the eyes when you speak to him. Show him you are not afraid of him and realize he is just doing his job. Through my own experience, if people were polite to me, I usually returned the courtesy, so be nice and cooperate!

Additionally, don't try to be too friendly with the officer or try to influence him in any way. Even if your uncle knows the officers Chief of Police. Most police officers do not like hearing about who a violator "knows", so don't use that line. Don't expect your police sticker that you have so cleverly put into plain view on the rear window of your car, to get you out of that ticket either. Additionally, never allow your passengers to converse with the officer, unless spoken to by the officer himself.

If you were stopped for a speeding violation, again, do not admit anything. You should be writing down or making some mental notes right about now. You should record for your own records, how fast you were really going at the time of the stop. Where did the officer come from, or where was his cruiser parked? What were the other traffic conditions in the area? Exactly where was your vehicle upon the roadway because you will need to return to this area at some point before court to make a diagram of the area and maybe take some photos. Also, make note of any weather problems, like rain, fog, etc. Note any bridges, radio towers, large signs, train tracks, high tension wires or anything else that stands out, which may have caused some type of interference with the radar. Taking photos of some of these objects may be wise also.

While I certainly do not advocate begging for a break from the law enforcement officer who has stopped you, I do caution you on choosing the proper approach in making that request should you choose to do it. Remember, most law enforcement officers have heard all the excuses before and usually are not swayed much by them. Further, by asking for a break, you are almost admitting your guilt. This is something I strongly recommend that you do not do, unless you really believe your excuse for speeding may get you off with maybe a warning. Unless you have no intention of fighting a speeding ticket should you receive one, then go ahead and ask for that break and provide the best excuse that you can think of. Make it good, remember, you are trying to get out of a ticket which carries a large fine.

Some of the better excuses that I have heard over the past 14 years in law enforcement are those which touch the heart. You may be able to use them because they did effect me. Those include the mother who has children in the vehicle, telling the officer that she can not afford a speeding ticket because the money that will go to pay the fine will come from the same money that is used to feed, cloth and shelter the children. This excuse works well because most police officers have families. Just be sure there are children, or signs that you have some, within the vehicle.

Another excuse that I found worked well, was a person asking for a break because they just found out from their doctor that they have terminal cancer, and to please not issue a ticket to them because it would only make their life more miserable and unbearable than it currently is. Try to show some sorrow and emotion and maybe tears, that would help get the point across. Tears by either sex work well, with a good excuse.

Should you decide, as I suggest, just to keep your mouth shut and go along with whatever the officer does, there are now some very important pieces of information that you MUST obtain to assist you in fighting and beating that ticket in a court of law.

In addition to what I have already told you, you must continue to document everything that is taking place. Seems like a lot of stuff to do, but in the long run it will be well worth it.

If the officer has used a speed detection device for basis of the actual stop, ask him some questions about the apprehension and equipment used. Some officers will invite the person back to observe the speed detection device within the cruiser. If you are offered this, do not refuse, get out and look at it. If you are not offered the chance to face or examine the evidence against you, ask to look at it. You are trying to find out the following very important pieces of information:

A. The make and model of the unit being used along with the serial numbers. Try to learn some things about the radar unit itself, like frequency band being used. Does the unit have "auto -lock" or "audio control" Doppler controls. As well as how often this radar unit is calibrated or maintained.

B. How it was used to obtain a reading, i.e.; stationary or moving mode. If moving mode was used, from which direction was the reading obtained? and how fast was the cruiser's speed at the time?

C. Ask the officer if tuning forks were used, and if so, obtain the tuning fork frequency and serial numbers also. This being if there are any in the cruiser.

D. Ask the officer about the "tracking history" and when and where he first observed your vehicle upon the roadway.

E. If radar was not used, ask the officer how long of a distance was he clocking your vehicle, and from what point to what point.

F. Obtain the cruiser plate and or car number that the officer was using because you will want to obtain the speedometer calibration and cruiser maintenance records of that particular car.

G. Ask the officer what his qualifications are as they pertain to the speed detection device he was operating at the time of your stop.

H. Obtain from the officer his full name, badge number and law enforcement agency, including his barracks number or letter if applicable. If two officers were involved in the stop, obtain the names and badge numbers of both. Be sure you know which officer performed which duty.

If you are allowed to look at the radar or other speed detection device, record the readings on it. Is it the speed that you are being charged with? Record the units model name, serial number and if applicable, the tuning fork frequencies and serial numbers. You should know though that members of law enforcement are usually not required to let you walk back to look at your speed.

Of course, not all members of law enforcement will cooperate with all of your requests for information. You will be met with a "Why do you want to know?" type of attitude in most cases. Remember, law enforcement looks at speeders as foes, or the "enemy" if you will and most will not be too cooperative with you. When you start to question them, you may very well succeed in catching the officer off guard an may actually stun him. Many officers write hundreds of tickets and never get challenged in any way by those motorists, so watch how he reacts to your questions. It may work in your favor. This is why your use of a mini-cassette recorder may be useful. Many courts will agree that a person should be allowed to see or face the evidence that is being used to convict them of a violation of the law. By being refused that opportunity can usually result in a dismissal of a speeding ticket with the help of a good lawyer.

Further, if that officer was rude, unpleasant or said anything unprofessional, the court may find you have a reasonable request for a dismissal. This may happen out of respect for that officer because if you went to trial, that officer might be very embarrassed by the text of those conversations. Even if the actual recording was not allowed, you could write down the text word for word, and present that to the court. The court may dismiss your ticket because of the way you were treated by the officer. So get that mini-recorder!!!

If you were not able to obtain some of the information that I suggested from the scene of the stop, don't worry too much. All you have to do is go into the police agency and request to see the records of the cruiser, the speed detection device as well as the arrest records of the arresting officer. You should also ask to see his certification records for operating that particular speed detection device. If you do not receive cooperation here on this level, the courts DA or prosecutor should be approached immediately and they should request that law enforcement agency provide those records that you or your attorney have requested.

Some additional pieces of information that you will need to gather either at the scene of the stop, or at a later time when you are preparing your diagram, is to locate the closest speed limit signs to the location of your stop. In many areas, you may not find a speed limit sign anywhere near the location of your vehicle stop. This itself could be very helpful in a court of law because many state courts have agreed that in order for a person to be convicted for a speeding violation, they have to first be warned about the speed limit for the area. The speed limit must be clearly posted and visible to the motorist traveling through that area. If there was no posted speed limit within miles of the location of your stop, you may have your ticket dismissed.

If you do receive a traffic ticket for a speeding violation or other type of traffic offense, I would advise you to sign the ticket if asked to do so. It shows a continuing effort on your part to cooperate with the officer, and thus, the entire system. A mere signing of a traffic ticket does not mean you are pleading guilty. It could just be a promise that you will appear in court to answer to the charge. In some areas, a failure to sign the ticket could result in you being taken into custody and arraigned before a traffic court immediately. This is not a wise thing to have happen because you will have had no chance to plan and prepare for your case in a court of law. Therefore, your odds of losing are great.

Once the motor vehicle stop has cleared, be sure before you leave that location you have most if not all of the information that you need for your case and the successful challenge of that speeding ticket in court.

Write down your version of what happened along with the date and time. If there were any witnesses or passenger inside your vehicle, have them prepare a written signed statement also.

If you have no time to make a diagram of the area at the time the stop is cleared, return to the same exact area as soon as possible. Draw the highway. Note everything that is important, like where your vehicle was within the roadway, where the other traffic was at the same time. Include bridge locations, power lines, guard rails, signs, radio towers and the approximate distances each was between the object and the location of the motor vehicle stop.

It also would be very helpful for you to return to the scene of the stop and take photographs or the area. This way you can prove obstacles, objects or other sources of interference that may have existed at the time the officer took a speed measurement reading of your vehicle. When the case finally gets to court, the officer may not even remember the stop and what, if any, such obstacles or objects existed there, along with the weather and traffic conditions.

One additional tip for you. In general, at the scene of the traffic stop, you are trying to touch the emotions of the officer by getting him down to your level as in person to person instead of officer to the offender or violator. This puts the officer more at ease and allows you the chance to converse with him, maybe even get him to laugh. This is very important, as well as maintaining eye contact with him at all times.

"Hello, High Risk Insurance Agency...Your yearly insurance rate for next year?...One moment please...Hmmm...well after reviewing all our records the very lowest going rate for your auto insurance for next year is... $5943.12"...

CLICK...

"Hello sir...hello?"

A conversation taking place in the near future should one continue to receive speeding tickets.

CHAPTER THREE

How to Fight that Ticket and WIN!

Most speeding tickets are given for speeds that are not extremely high or excessive. Many are issued to drivers who are operating at or slightly above the general flow of traffic. This is usually operating between 10-15 mph in excess of the posted speed limit of 55 mph, which, according to the National Highway Traffic Safety Administration, are speeds at which the fewest accidents occur!

Most people, over half according to some studies, pay their ticket fines instead of appealing them and going to court. Some experts estimate that between 15-20%, and as high as 30%, of all speeding tickets are given or issued in error if radar is the speed detection device used. There are many reasons for these errors, including inadequate operator training, interference from roadside objects or the reading of a speed from the wrong vehicle.

For many people, the mere thought of appealing a speeding ticket and having to appear in a court of law to present their case, produces fear, anxiety and a lot of resistance. Nobody really likes having to go to court for any reason, let alone, traffic court. Some motorists feel that because they have exceeded the speed limits many times before, without getting stopped and ticketed, that this time they deserved the ticket they received. They may feel an obligation to pay the fine, and many do so without any kind of fight or appeal. These people forget about the insurance surcharges and the impact speeding ticket convictions have on ones driving record.

Many other people feel fighting a speeding ticket is just a waste of time because all that will happen is that they will be found guilty. They will then have to pay a fine and in some instances, lose a days pay from work. It is these people who feel that the court will side with the police officer, and because they believe police radar to be infallible. Others just fear the thought of losing and being embarrassed. For whatever the reason, I will change the mind of many of those people, and convince everybody that the odds are in their favor of winning their case in traffic court.

SHOULD YOU FIGHT THAT SPEEDING TICKET? AND WHY?

In my opinion, the answer to that question is YES! Everybody should consider fighting a speeding ticket that they have received and should go to court and present a defense on their behalf. This is why you bought the book, right? You want to learn how you can fight a speeding ticket in court and win.

Remember, speed enforcement on the highways and roads in the United States are generally fiscally and politically inspired and motivated. And the myth makers want you to believe that radar and laser are infallible. Remember, no speed detection or enforcement device is free from mistakes or error. I have already gone into a lot of detail in explaining to you the many flaws and weaknesses associated with the speed detection devices being used by law enforcement today. Further, the National Highway Traffic Safety

Administration and the National Bureau of Standards, have extensively tested several different models and brands of police radar and found many errors, so many that their reports indicate that police radar could be considered unreliable and inaccurate at times.

For many average, law abiding American citizens, a minor traffic offense like speeding, will be the only traffic law they may ever break in their entire lives. Yet, because of the greed of the system, these people will be penalized for up to three years, or more. First they will pay the excessively high fine to the town, city or state where they received the speeding ticket in. Then, they will fall mercy to the insurance companies whom seek surcharge moneys and higher premiums. The average speeding ticket, with all fines and insurance penalties will cost a person about $1,000.00. If this unfortunate person has more than one or two speeding tickets on his driving record history, that amount could exceed $2,500.00 over the course of a three year period. Yet, this is exactly what occurs thousands of times a day in every state across America.

On top of the fines and insurance surcharges, a persons driving record will fall victim if they get convicted of a speeding violation. Most if not all Department of Motor Vehicles in each state, keep track of a persons driving record and history, usually under a point system. If a person has received too many traffic tickets, and thus, too many points on their driving record, the DMV may suspend or revoke a persons license for a specific length of time. Then they may charge that person an excessive amount of money to have their license reinstated.

To answer that question of why fight a speeding ticket and go to court, I say to save money in fines and insurance surcharges, as well as to protect ones driving record. It could also just be for the principle that one wants to fight a speeding ticket in court. Many people are bothered by the fact that the system focuses more on making money by issuing speeding tickets, than for public safety. Another reason to fight the ticket is because radar itself and its operators are not foolproof or free from errors.

WHAT ARE THE CHANCES OF WINNING IN COURT?

By reading this book, you are now armed with more knowledge than some lawyers or even the police themselves, in mounting a successful challenge against a speeding ticket in a court of law.

This is a book about winning. There will undoubtedly be some things that I will tell you to do that some may find to be somewhat unreasonable, but none of the strategies, tips or tactics that I tell you about are considered illegal. Remember, your sole purpose for purchasing this book is to win in court, and beat that traffic ticket. Regardless of how my advice may strike you, it should be considered anyway because it could be that one thing you do or don't do, that makes, or breaks your case.

Winning itself takes on many definitions, it is how you yourself define winning that is most important. Successfully beating a speeding ticket in a court of law has not generally been an easy thing to do. If a person has been successful in lowering their total fine this could be considered a win to some people, and a loss to others.

There are some things one should consider to be wins in their fight to beat a speeding ticket. These include the fact that because you have read this book, you now know what to do, and what not to do, when you are stopped for a speeding violation. Further, by pleading not guilty, you are taking a stand, and did not just pay the ticket and not fight back. You may be successful in getting the ticket dismissed which will save you money because there will be no fines to pay, no insurance surcharges or premium increases, as well as keeping ones driving record clean.

The basic principle in our criminal justice system is that a person is innocent until proven guilty, unless they have been stopped for speeding that is. You see, the system expects people who have received a speeding ticket to plead guilty and send in the fine.

There are some things going in your favor though. First, prosecutors or district attorneys do not like trials for speeding tickets, so many will attempt to plea bargain with you. By going to court and pleading not guilty, one can expect to receive the offer of a reduced fine or charge, or less points on ones driving record. To some, this could be considered a "win", and to others this could be a "loss" because they wanted the ticket thrown out of court completely.

Second, should your case come up before a judge, there is a good chance, if you can raise some reasonable doubt in your case, the judge (the majority of which are fair and honest men and women) may dismiss or lower the charge or fine amount for you. Your success will depend on how persuasive you have been with that judge or prosecutor on the reliability of the speed detection device and how competent you looked to them. If a person is willing to take the time to prepare themselves, study the speed detection device that was used to obtain a speed reading on their vehicle, along with a good presentation of the facts and doubts of a case, the chances are pretty good that you will be successful in some manner in court.

You need to be aware though, that this book is only to be used as a guide. Each case carries its own set of facts and circumstances and laws are different in every state. It is your responsibility to check with your own states laws and procedures as they pertain to speeding tickets and fighting them in a court of law.

Winning a trial in court can be difficult. Remember, you are in a court of law, going against the system itself. Police officers are trained that every time they write a speeding ticket, they are ridding the roadways of a menace. Hence, that police officer may do whatever he has to do to get a conviction in court, and make his ticket stick. This may include bending the truth. The officer may state he made a visual observation of a vehicle and estimated its speed prior to verifying with a speed detection device. He may further state he observed other traffic in the area of your vehicle but will state he is sure he picked up your vehicle on his speed detection device. He may also say he calibrated a radar unit with tuning forks before and after every stop, when in fact, he did not.

From my own experience, most police officers do not use the tuning forks before and after every motor vehicle stop, I know that I did not most of the time. You have to be prepared for this type of testimony in court. You have to hope you have an open minded judge or prosecutor and must be able to seize any opportunity or opening in the case, should one be given, to make your case strong, and convincing. Most judges will accept the testimony of police officers especially if backed by a speed detection device. You must stand up in court and proclaim your innocence. You must raise doubts about the speed detection device used and tell the court about the units flaws, sources of interference and other deficiencies. Question the qualifications of the law enforcement officer operating the equipment. You must create doubt in any way to convince a judge to dismiss the case. You need to be strong, convinced, polite, poised and respectful at all times. Above all, don't be afraid. The system is there to work for and with you. If you do not attempt to challenge the speeding ticket, you have already lost.

DO YOU NEED A LAWYER?

This is a personal preference or choice. This book is designed to assist a person who decides to go to court alone, without a lawyer, to challenge their traffic ticket and win at fighting it. That is why I wrote this book.

If a person can afford a lawyer or attorney, one may wish to consider hiring one. They can be very helpful in getting through some of the red tape associated with being in a court of law. This includes any plea bargaining that may go on between the state and yourself. An attorney may be useful if your case can be dismissed because of some legal procedure or other challenge.

Like any other professional, choose your attorney carefully. Many consider traffic court to be trivial and they may not be the best attorney to have representing you in that case. Find an attorney who specializes in traffic court violations.

An organization entitled the National Motorists Association whom can be reached at 1-608-849-6000, is a national legal referral service for traffic related offenses. Membership is required in this organization and if a person has been a member for over one year and has renewed their membership, this organization will pay for their ticket in court should they not be successful in beating it for their member. What a win-win situation this is! Joining this organization may be a wise thing to do if you find yourself in traffic court too often. Their website is www.motorists.com, check it out.

PREPARING YOUR DEFENSE CASE

The key to winning your case in traffic court, is to show that the speed detection device or the law enforcement officer operating it, made an error of some kind. As I already have mentioned, there are many flaws with the various speed detection devices being used by law enforcement today. This coupled with the training and qualifications of the officers using the equipment, sometimes can present a clear case of reasonable doubt for that traffic ticket in court.

Even if you were in fact actually speeding, and you got stopped and issued a speeding ticket, you need to fight that ticket in a court of law. You may have been issued that ticket by a radar unit that was not working properly or being operated by an unqualified operator. It is because of these kinds of reasons that a speeding ticket may get thrown out of court. If you purchased this book, you must have been interested in learning how to fight that speeding ticket. Use some of my strategies, tips and tactics and go to court and fight it. You really have little to lose and so very much to gain.

To launch a successful attack on a speeding ticket in a court of law a person must be prepared. You must fully establish and lay out before the court all of the circumstances under which the traffic stop was made and the subsequent speeding ticket issued. The burden of proof is on the state to prove that you are guilty of speeding. You, however, need to offer to the court any reasonable alternative to the officers version of the traffic stop. To assist you in preparing for court, you need to follow everything that I have explained to you in Chapter Two, on the motor vehicle stop itself. This is because my friends, your successful challenge to a police radar issued speeding ticket starts here, with the actual stop.

Once you have been issued a speeding ticket, and have followed the advice given in Chapter Two, pertaining to the actual stop. You need to take that ticket and send in a "Not Guilty" plea, and are requesting a hearing before a court magistrate, prosecutor or judge. You need to do this immediately because on most tickets there are dates that a ticket must be turned in by, whether a person pays the fine or pleads "not guilty" and has asked for a hearing. You will be notified, usually through the mail, of when your court date will be held and at what court. If the speed you were charged with was excessive, you may be sent to court automatically, with a trial date already set. It is not likely the arresting officer will be there on that day, so once in court, plead not guilty and ask for a trial.

As advised in Chapter Two, you need to have a complete description of the area where you were stopped. Take photos and make a map if necessary. Note the power lines, bridge and overpasses, large signs, television or cable antennas, radar stations, airplanes and trains. You are trying to show there may have been some electromagnetic interference in the area at the time of the stop. And in court, you will need to prove the existence of these items.

Fighting a speeding ticket in a court of law and winning is not an impossible task. Magistrates, prosecutors and judges are used to hearing these kinds of cases and if a person comes before them prepared, polite, sure and confident of their defense, many court officers, including the judge himself, may go out of their way to help, offer little or no resistance, and may even find someone not guilty and dismiss the speeding ticket.

Of course, a person who follows the guidelines of this book, who then retains the services of a competent traffic attorney, may stand a little better chance of being successful in a court of law. Attorneys usually are better able to speak to the court official directly. The lawyer may be better able to raise doubts about the workings of the police radar, the operators qualifications or any other issues found to be helpful in winning your case. The choice to present a case in court on ones own, or to hire a competent attorney, rests with the person them self.

Should one decide to go it alone, this book will be very helpful, that was my hope in writing it. My book will help you take advantage of some of the provisions of the law, like the right to represent yourself in court, to face your accuser and to see the evidence that the state has against you. Of course, in order to be successful, one must be prepared, know their facts and all of the issues pertaining to the speed detection device and the actual motor vehicle stop.

One interesting point to keep in mind when fighting a speeding ticket, is that in many states, the officer who issued the ticket must appear in court. He must testify about the facts concerning the actual motor vehicle stop. Many times, the officer will not show up, for a number of reasons. He could be just unavailable, on vacation, or be out sick from work. Many officers feel that going to court on a speeding ticket case is a waste of time and most hate it too!! If the officer does not appear in court, a ticket may be dismissed, but the officer himself may not really be concerned with that. It may even be a good idea to attempt to find out when the arresting officer is on vacation and attempt to schedule the trial during that time. Call the officer's department and ask when the officer is planning his vacation. Some dispatchers will give this information out if it is known to them. Its worth the phone call, so try it. The officer will most likely not show up in court if he is in fact on vacation. Many people have won their cases in court because of reasons like this. If the officer is not present, the case is usually dismissed.

GATHERING YOUR EVIDENCE

As part of the preparation in building your case for a successful defense in court, there are some important pieces of information that you must obtain prior to going to court. Some of this information will act as "evidence" for your defense.

You will need to get the following records from the law enforcement agency whose officer stopped you. All of these records should be available for public review, and available right at that agency. Should you encounter difficulty in obtaining any of this information, contact the clerk of the court or the prosecutor and inform them of that difficulty. The court may elect to issue a subpoena to that law enforcement agency, which requires them to turn the requested information over to either the court itself, or you.

<u>IMPORTANT RECORDS TO OBTAIN</u>

1. Copies of all the manufacturer's specifications for the radar itself, or other speed detection device being challenged. Also obtain all training, operator and technical manuals for that particular speed detection unit.

2. Any daily use, calibration and testing logs for the speed detection device.

3. All service and maintenance records for that particular speed detection device, along with its tuning forks if applicable and those records of accuracy and testing. Some departments require daily tuning fork logs be filled out.

4. The arresting officers arrest records for previous year, along with those from the day of your stop.

5. The arresting officers certification, training records and quali-fications for the radar or other speed detection device that was used to back up his stop of you and the subsequent issuance of a speeding ticket.

6. All repair records of the patrol unit used by the arresting offi-cer, along with the certification for calibration of that cruisers speedometer.

7. The agency's FCC (Federal Communications Commission) license, which authorized their radar use.

If you are not successful in obtaining these records from the law enforcement agency, or through the court having jurisdiction, make sure on the day of your trial, you let the magistrate or judge hear-ing your case know about this. Then make a motion to dismiss the case based on your inability to review the requested records and documents that would have helped you present a proper and fair defense case. In some instances you will prevail, in others, your case will be postponed until the state obtains the information requested and turns it over to you.

Now that you have these documents, what do they mean and what do you do with them?? First, study them all and try to find any problem with any of the records or documents. Then target that area for your defense. Keep in mind that there may be some other areas other than those listed, that one may target for a challenge in court.

For example, the area in which you were stopped was not properly posted with the speed limit, as required by the vehicle code in some states. Another may be that the officer made errors on the traffic ticket itself, like an improper or inaccurate date, time, location of alleged offense, or the name and address of the offender was wrong. These could all be used as successful challenges, they might pro-vide reasonable doubt as to the accuracy and reliability of the arresting officer.

In reviewing the documents that you have obtained from the law enforcement agency, be sure that you have been provided all that have been requested. If anything is missing, make a note of it.

Serial #
device

In examining the records of the radar unit or other speed detection device, first check the serial number. You want to make sure that the number matches that of the unit being used by the officer who stopped you. If the numbers do not match, there could be grounds for an immediate dismissal.

maint.
log of
device

Check the units repair and maintenance logs and records. Has the unit been repaired often? Has it been calibrated and checked as per state laws, if applicable? Some departments keep very sloppy logs, and records, which could be helpful to your case. A unit that has been repaired often or recently could be inaccurate or unreliable, and may raise that reasonable doubt to the court official. A unit that has never been sent out for a check, or calibration could also present some reasonable doubt to the court. Be aware however, that unless you uncover something concrete, like a radar unit having been repaired just days before your stop, don't plan to use the maintenance records in your defense because it could do more harm than good.

Be sure to check my chart in the Appendix section (in the back of this book) and check your own states laws as they pertain to speed detection device certification and types of devices used. Some states also require year or twice yearly inspection and calibrations of all units and their tuning forks.

Tuning
Fork

Along with the police radar, are its tuning forks. Again, check the records given to you to be sure that the serial numbers match with the forks used in your original stop, if this is known. Check the certificate of calibration and accuracy. If there is no certificate, some states will dismiss a ticket based on the tuning fork not being traceable to a given standard.

Another area of the obtained records and documents that you will really want to go over thoroughly, is that of the arresting officer. Has the officer had the 24 hours of classroom training and the 16 hours of supervised field use, as recommended by the National Highway Traffic Safety Administration? A mere certificate stating the officer is "qualified" may not hold too much weight in court once you question why there is no NHTSA training certificate, or records indicating some retraining during the past 5 years (as also recommended by the NHTSA). Be sure the records you receive for the officer qualify or certify him in the use and operation of that speed detection device.

Additionally, in checking the arrest records of the arresting officer for the past year, look for a pattern of speeding ticket arrests for the area in which you were stopped and ticketed. In some states an area of high ticket issuance could be considered a "speed trap" and may be illegal. Also, some judges may not like police officers whom routinely ticket people in the same area over and over for speeds considered safe and reasonable. Don't however, expect much in this area that would help you.

You will also need to check the maintenance records of the patrol cruiser, along with the speedometer calibration and certification. Does that cruiser have a history of electrical problems which could in turn, cause interference with the radar or other speed detection device? Has the speedometer been checked to be accurate and reliable on a regular basis as required by law in some states? This is very important if an officer "clocked" or followed you and issued you a speeding ticket based on his readings of his cruiser speedometer.

Finally, every law enforcement agency that uses radar must first have a license issued to them by the Federal Communications Commission. If that agency does not have such a license, your ticket may be dismissed in court. On that FCC license, will be the list of models, makes and serial numbers for the units that agency is authorized to use. If the unit that was used to issue you your speeding ticket is not on that list, that agency can not use that radar units information against you.

What information have you been able to uncover that may help you in court? No matter what it may be, or how minor it may seem, make note of it and write it down. Every piece of information that you obtain for your defense could be the key to winning your case in court.

General
info

You need to keep in mind that your version of what really happened in that motor vehicle stop, must be based on facts that are both believable and acceptable to the court. You can not just wander into court and present some half thought out theory of why your vehicle was not responsible for the speed reading the officer took the day of the stop.

Remember, between the many flaws and weaknesses that exist with every speed detection device, coupled with inadequate operator training and experience, you may be able to prove to the court that there is reasonable doubt surrounding your speeding ticket. As you begin to read further you will learn more on raising reasonable doubt, and why it is so important in wining your case.

YOUR FIRST DAY IN COURT

Congratulations for making it this far. You already have won the battle of fear just by coming to court to present a defense in your case.

Your first day in court can be considered to be your arraignment day. On the day that you are required to appear for your hearing, you will be informed of the charge against you, and will be asked how you plead. Of course, your response will be "not guilty". In some states, your hearing will be before a clerk-magistrate, or a judge. You will be allowed to hear the facts as presented by either the arresting officer himself, or an officer designated to represent his agency at the arraignment. You will then present your rebuttal or defense version of the facts. That clerk-magistrate will make a decision of your guilt or innocence based on the facts and circumstances that were just presented to them. If you are found guilty or responsible, ask for a trial by judge or jury if applicable in your state. A trial by judge is preferred because jury trials are expensive, time consuming and not usually granted in speeding ticket cases. A judge may be more reasonable and fair and flexible in dismissing your case or lowering the fine or charge. You will then be allowed to leave court and will be notified of the trial date.

Of course, you may have been successful and had your ticket thrown out, dismissed, or reduced to a lesser charge or smaller fine. All of these can be considered wins.

Some general pointers one should know prior to going to court include the most obvious. One should be there on time, and if you can't make your court date, notify the court immediately and request a continuance. In some states, no continuances will be granted and should you fail to show up for the hearing, you may be found guilty or responsible for the charge. In some areas of the country a bench warrant for your arrest for default, or not showing up as instructed, may be issued. Do everything possible to be there on the required day, date and time. Of course, dress in a suit and tie and look professional. Always be polite and address the judge as " *Your Honor*" and the police officer as *"Officer"*. Maintain your composure at all times, in other words, stay in control.

Additionally, in any court hearing you have concerning your attempt to beat a traffic ticket, you should always tell the clerk-magistrate or judge, that you lost a full days pay to come to court and present your case. This shows the court how strong you are in your conviction to beat the ticket by presenting a believable and acceptable excuse or defense in the case. It also will show your monetary loss to the court who may be more willing to reduce or dismiss your traffic ticket fine or charge.

In some jurisdictions, you may be required to have your trial that very day, after arraignment, if you were found guilty or responsible. Be prepared for this and have your case ready to present should it become necessary. Also, any passengers within your vehicle at the time of the traffic stop, whom may be used as a witness in court, should accompany you. Most judges will grant a continuance however, allowing additional time to prepare your case for court.

In this chapter, you will learn how to present your case before the court. You will be given some generalized sample question material to ask of the arresting officer, who will have to take the stand and tell their case, provided you have progressed this far. If you simply are in a hearing with a clerk-magistrate, this may not be possible. You will only be able to plead guilty, guilty with an explanation, or not guilty. You may or may not be found responsible or guilty, so request the trial by judge.

You will also learn how to present the plausible errors on the various speed detection devices that we have discussed throughout this book thus far. These include police radar, laser, photo radar, Vascar and clocking. By presenting these possible errors as explanations of why your speeding ticket was issued unjustly, you may create reasonable doubt in the eyes of the court.

Many of you reading this book, are going to follow my advice and plead not guilty, sending the speeding ticket into the proper official agency, requesting a hearing in court as to your guilt or innocence. Some of you will still elect to pay their fines, for whatever reason, For those of you who plead not guilty, and ask for a court hearing, it is at that hearing you will then be asked to enter another plea. A guilty plea is acknowledging to the court that you committed the violation and are ready to accept the punishment for it, be it a fine or whatever. A not guilty plea is a plea of innocence, stating that you do not believe you are guilty of the violation you are charged with and you want the court to hear your case and determine your guilt or innocence. Upon the decision of the court, you agree to accept that decision. A plea of *"no contest"* is allowed in some jurisdictions also. This is like a plea of guilty, but without actually admitting your guilt. This plea is helpful in that your plea is not an admission of guilt, therefore, it can not be used against you in a civil trial of some kind. There is another plea that many people may choose to enter, that is *"guilty with an explanation"*.

GUILTY WITH AN EXPLANATION

Although I do not recommend a person go to court and plead guilty to a violation of the law that they were arrested for, there are some people who feel that by going to court and pleading guilty, that they can "explain" the reason for that violation. This is done in the attempt to find some sympathy from either the clerk-magistrate, prosecutor or judge. Although this may work in some cases, it is indeed very risky because a person could loose completely and will have wasted a lot of time and money (including the money spent to purchase this book!).

A person who has decided to proceed with a guilty plea, and intends to present an explanation or an excuse to the court as to why they may have been speeding, needs to remember, that the courts have heard a lot of different excuses from people. Make sure your excuse is believable and convincing. It also needs to be presented in a sharp, and confident manner.

You should first, as mentioned earlier, inform the hearing officer, clerk-magistrate, prosecutor or judge, that you lost a full days pay in order to come to court to present your explanation of defense in the case.

If you elect to admit to speeding, don't admit the speed to the court. By not admitting the actual speed you were traveling, the court may be more inclined to plea bargain with you and lower the fine total or the actual charge. All you need to tell the court is that you may have been exceeding the speed limit, but are not sure by how much, and that you do not believe it was as fast as the arresting officer stated.

Explanations

After listening to you explain that the weather was clear, no other vehicles or pedestrians were on the roadway or in the area, and that you were in fact operating at a safe and reasonable speed, even though you were doing 45 mph in a 35 mph zone, the court official may dismiss the case.

One of the better explanations that can be used, is that your vehicle speedometer was not working properly. In order to back that up, get a friend who is a mechanic to write up a repair slip indicating that work was done to correct the malfunctioning speedometer. Have the cost of the repair exceed $100.00. This once again shows the court how much money you have already lost in this endeavor to beat the speeding ticket.

There are many other excuses that one may consider using when they go to court. I will not go into any detail because everybody has their own reason for why they were speeding. I do not recommend this type of tactic because it usually is not very successful unless the explanation or excuse is very believable and appears to be valid and true.

DEVELOP YOUR STRATEGIES

Your courtroom defense plan needs to be worked out well in advance of court. You may only have one opportunity to present a defense to that traffic ticket. Know the strengths and weaknesses of your case as much as possible. You need to develop and choose your weapon or what you will do in court to bring about reasonable doubt that may trigger a dismissal of your traffic ticket.

State needs to...

The state will have to show a few things in their case in order to obtain a conviction against you. They will have to show that the speed detection device was working properly, was calibrated, as well as the tuning forks, that the officer was competent to operate that device, the cruise speedometer was accurate, and that the officer had proper jurisdiction in the area where on a certain date and time, he observed you operating in excess of the posted speed limit which he backed up with the speed detection device. Additionally, that agency has a license to operate that speed detection device with the Federal Communications Commission.

You will need to decide what to attack and develop your defense around that area. It could be the officer certification or training, the cruiser speedometer etc. Whatever you found out by obtaining and examining the records from that law enforcement agency who stopped you, should be used in your defense. Refer back to page 52 under the heading "Important Records to Obtain", for further information on review of the records.

THE STATE'S CASE AGAINST YOU

By now, you probably have gone to the initial hearing at the court, and you have been found guilty or responsible for the traffic ticket you are now fighting. You have now returned to court for your trial. In some jurisdictions, your arraignment and trial may take place the very same day or may even be the same thing in some courts. Whatever the case may be, you are in court and the trial against you is about to begin.

By this time, you should be prepared, complete with any passengers who will act as a witness for you, your diagram or maps, photos of the area, documents and records from the police department. You should have your defense strategy ready in every aspect and have all of your facts straight.

You will, at some point, have your name called, and the trial will begin. The state or prosecution will present their case first.

officers
Testimony

Usually, in most courts, the arresting officer will testify first. He will present his side of the story. The officer will first state his name, his police department or agency, and proceed into telling the court the date and time of the violation and where it was committed. He will also state the type of speed detection device used and the manufacturer. The officer will normally include how the unit was calibrated and what he observed prior to stopping your vehicle. He will say he observed your vehicle traveling in excess of the posted speed and that the speed detection device confirmed this. Subsequently a traffic stop was made and a ticket issued for speeding.

Take
notes

When the officer is telling his story, pay attention and make notes if necessary. The officer may have left out something you consider important. He may not even recall the stop and be ad-libbing his testimony. You can bring this to the attention of the judge if it is important to your case.

The states case is pretty simple, basic and straightforward. The prosecutor or district attorney may ask the officer some additional questions concerning the traffic stop, like how it was made, what were the weather conditions, etc. The states case does not last too long.

My turn to
ask
Questions

You will now be given an opportunity to ask the arresting officer himself some questions. Believe it or not, this will make the officer nervous. Most members of law enforcement are not used to being challenged, let alone in court, by a person whom they have arrested. This can work to your advantage if you pick up on it.

You will need to target several areas during your cross-examination of the police officer. Remember, he is just a person like yourself and try not to be too afraid or intimidated by asking him questions. Many do find this task difficult because the officer is usually in uniform.

You will need to target the following:

A. Was a tracking history taken by the Officer, and was he tracking the right vehicle.

B. Did the offense take place in an area where the speed limit changed close to where you were stopped.

C. Are there errors in the evidence against you, namely the speeding ticket.

D. The failure of the officer to detect and avoid spurious speed readings from non target sources, or a weather condition existed that should have rendered the speed detection device unreliable.

E. The speed detection device itself, tuning forks if applicable and its flaws and weak points. Included would be the maintenance, calibration and accuracy documents.

F. The qualifications and competency of the officer who is operating that speed detection device.

G. The police cruiser speedometer calibration certificates.

H. The law enforcement agency was FCC licensed.

I. If inclimate weather, hot or cold, target if the cruiser's A/C or defrosters were "on" during the time of your traffic stop, because both interefere with radar operation.

Every traffic stop is different, and carries its own set of facts and circumstances, the choice of what kind of defense a person decides to bring in court, is up to them. One stop may have occurred near several high tension wires. Others may have occurred in the rain. Additionally, in reviewing the records and documents requested form the law enforcement agency, there could be any number of problems found in the review of these documents, as we have earlier discussed. It is up to you to choose which defense strategy you will use.

General
strategies

Remember, that strategy could be as simple as errors on your speed ticket, the failure to possess or use tuning forks for calibration, having no certificate that qualifies the officer to be operating that speed detection device, or the issuance of a speed ticket based purely on observations and no speed detection device readings to back that observation up.

CROSS-EXAMINING THE OFFICER

Remember the basics as you begin. Stay calm, be polite, address the judge as "Your Honor" and the officer as "Officer" and it is very important to sound sure, positive and to remain in complete control.

officer's
presence
in court

You should know, that in many cases, the arresting officer does not show up in court, and for a variety of reasons. If this happens, your case is usually dismissed immediately. Also, if two officers are involved in your speeding ticket arrest, such as one was operating the radar and the other stopped you and issued the ticket, both have

Q's To ask
↓

to appear in court. One officer can not testify about actions of another, that is called hearsay and is not allowed in court.

1ST Q:

Your initial series of questions to the officer will elicit the basic information from him, such as name, department, type of speed detection device being used and what mode it was in, what he observed prior to stopping your vehicle, why he stopped your vehicle, and what are the qualifications of the officer to operate the speed detection device. All of these can be asked of the officer and will usually be answered truthfully.

2nd a:

Now is the time you will target the area of your defense that will produce a reasonable doubt in the courts eyes, as to the issuance of your speeding ticket. This will depend on what area you choose to target.

If you were issued a ticket that contained errors on it, bring this to the attention of the officer and court. This is always a good way to get to the officer, by showing him he made mistakes, it also keeps the judges eyes open.

Ⓐ Ask the officer, if he issued a ticket based on observation only and no speed detection device reading. If he did do this ask him why, and then ask how he can be sure of the actual speed. This should help shed some reasonable doubt in the court, all to your favor.

Ⓑ Question the officer to see if he took a tracking history, if he even knows what one is. Then ask him to explain how he took that tracking history, and how he picked your vehicle as the target. This is very important because the beam of radar, for example, can only pick up a vehicles speed. If there was more than one vehicle in the general area, the officer has to now testify as to how he is sure your vehicle was the correct target which registered the speed reading.

Ⓒ If there was a weather problem, like rain, snow, fog, etc. , ask the officer why he was operating a speed detection device in inclement weather, and if he is aware most speed detection devices produce far more false speed readings in that kind of foul weather.

Ⓓ Should there have been some large object in the area, like bridges, radio towers, large signs, train tracks, high tension wires, question the officer first, as to the existence of those items, and if he was aware they existed in the location of the traffic stop. Continue on asking the officer if he is aware that such objects very often produce false readings. If you have diagrams and photos of these items, show them to the arresting officer as well as the judge.

Ⓔ If you plan to challenge the speed detection device itself, target the area you feel would present a reasonable doubt in the eyes of the court. For example, did the unit just recently get repaired?, or has it been repaired frequently? Has it been calibrated and certified as required by state law? Were tuning forks used and if so, were they accurate and calibrated yearly? Remember, you will have obtained a lot of information at the scene of the stop, if you followed my guidelines. You should already know if the officer even had tuning forks in the cruiser. Ask the officer if he offered to let you look at the speed detection device being used by himself that day.

(E) In questing the officer about police radar, ask him if he is aware of false speed readings being given because of the cruiser A/C unit, CB radios. Ask him if he is familiar with the terms "shadowing", "bumping" and "batching". If he states he is, ask him to explain them to the court. If he does not, you explain them to him and ask him if he agrees. Also cover when 2 or more vehicles are in the radar beam, it is difficult to pick which vehicle is the correct target. I have already explained all of these things to you in Chapter One, so you should already be familiar with them, and should be using that knowledge to your benefit.

(G) Bring to the courts attention, that at the scene of the traffic stop, the officer refused to let you inspect the speed detection device, the speed shown which, according to the officer, was your speed, the tuning forks used, (if applicable) along with other important information you feel you had a right to see which would have assisted you. Tell the court that you believe you have a right to confront and examine the evidence that the state will use against you. This includes an inspection of the speed detection device.

(H) You should further state to the court that you recorded that conversation pertaining to the arresting officer refusing to let you look at the speed detection device. State that you recorded every conversation that took place. Use this tactic if the officer was rude or did something unprofessional in your overall defense. The court may not allow this to be admissible, but you will certainly have created some reasonable doubt, in addition to totally embarrassing the officer.

(I) You should also question the officer as to why he did certain things at the scene of the stop. Ask him why he was refusing to let you look at the speed detection device, or why he was rude, etc. He must answer these questions in court, and may not be prepared to do so.

J) Should you review the officers training and qualification records, on his competency to operate that certain speed detection device, ask him to tell the court about his training. You will need to ask the officer who trained him, where he was trained, how many hours of training he received, and when was the last refresher course he attended. With any luck, the officer will not have had much training. It is at this time you make it known to the officer and the court, that the National Highway Traffic Safety Administration in February of 1980, issued recommendations to law enforcement on the training standards for speed detection devices. Further state that the NHTSA requires 24 hours of classroom training along with 16 hours of supervised field training, and that they also recommend a refresher course every 1 to 3 years. This line of questioning could cast doubt on the officers expertise and may help establish reasonable doubt.

K) Should your speeding ticket be issued based on a "pacing" or "clocking" by that officer, and your records have indicated that the particular cruisers speedometer has not been calibrated at least once yearly, ask the officer about this. It should help show the court that the cruiser speedometer may not be reliable or accurate.

L) A patrol car that has had a series of electrical problems as found in your review of the maintenance records of that particular cruiser, may indicate an electrical problem, which could provide interference with a speed detection device, and thus, a false speed reading. Further, the cruisers electrical system may not have given a stable power source, also cause for an unreliable and false speed reading.

Your exact line of questioning will depend on the hypotheses you adopt in your defense. And I have already touched on many of them. Use this information to question the arresting officer about every aspect of the traffic stop.

laser

(m)

If Laser or Vascar speed detection units were used, refer back to those chapters. Review the data presented and attack those units by asking the officer questions that revolve around the unit. Find out if these speed detection devices are accepted in your state as reliable and accurate by the courts. Challenge the training and qualifications of the arresting officer also. Raise all of the points I have already explained about the weaknesses of these speed detection devices.

I can not present every question that you need to ask the arresting officer here. That would be almost impossible. As mentioned earlier, every case is different and so is every approach to dealing with a speeding ticket in court. I can not try to make you a lawyer either just by reading this book. Proper preparation for your defense will require some work on your part, but compared to the gains should you be successful in court and win at beating your ticket, that time spent in preparation would have been well worth it!

(n)

Finally, question the officer as to the existence of an FCC license for his agency, if you have found in your search for records, that the agency does not have one. Or that a certain speed detection device is not listed on the license. As I have mentioned before, every law enforcement agency is required to have the FCC license if operating speed detection devices.

I should probably mention something that through my own experience, happens quite often when members of law enforcement have to go to court and testify. Many officers, in order to obtain a conviction, may "lie" or fudge the truth in certain areas. Most officers will state they calibrated a radar unit with a tuning fork before and after every stop, when in fact they did not. Many will state without any doubt, that they accurately picked your vehicle as the target vehicle being speed monitored by a speed detection device, when in fact, they may have only guessed and picked your vehicle out of others in the same general vicinity being monitored. Be on the guard for this and expect it to occur. It is, sad to admit, very common in law enforcement.

o s/ns

Once you feel as though you have raised the points most important in your case, inform the court you have no more questions for the officer. The prosecution may now redirect or re-question the officer. He will be trying to repair any damage that you have caused in this case. Be on the watch for leading questions or the attempt to present any new subject or line of questioning that was not already covered in either his direct or your cross-examination of the arresting officer. You also have the right to re-cross the officer should it be necessary.

.l use officer

If you are confident that you have raised the points you feel to be most important in your examination of the arresting officer, excuse him, and call any witness to the stand now. A witness in your case should only be there for one reason, and that is to state to the court that you were not speeding. They can also back up your theory or hypothesis about your traffic stop, whatever it is that you used in your defense. Be sure that person testifies that you were driving safe and reasonable. Get that information out and dismiss your witness. Of course, the prosecution does get to ask that witness some questions, but, if they do, it is usually brief and to the point. Just be sure your witness is ready for that and does not provide anything more than asked for.

SHOULD YOU TESTIFY?

In most cases, you will be conducting your trial before a judge and not a jury. Therefore, it usually does not require you to testify in your own behalf. After all, you are already acting as your own defense attorney. All you would be testifying about anyway is that you are not guilty. If you take the stand, the state has the opportunity to ask you questions, and that is a situation I recommend a person not get themselves into. If you were testifying before a jury, where you may attempt to win their sympathy, taking the stand would be advised. A judge is less likely to think anything negative if a person elects not to testify in their own case. A jury on the other hand, may think a person is trying to hide something by not testifying in their own behalf. Taking to the stand is therefore, not advised. Enter your plea before the court and present your best defense case, and final argument and sit down and await the judges decision.

MAKE A MOTION TO DISMISS

Once the prosecution and yourself are finished with the officer, and witness, the court may ask you if you have anything further. It is at this time you may consider asking for a dismissal based on any number of things.

One can make a motion for dismissal on any of the following:

I.   The Citation contained errors thus, showing the officer was less than attentive.

II. The area where you were stopped for speeding was not clearly posted with the speed limit.

III. The police have not yet provided some of the requested records and documents, thus not allowing me to present a solid case. This is because information of possible problems with the speed detection device, arresting officer or the patrol unit have been withheld.

IV. The officers testimony revealed some flaws in the operation of the speed detection device by that officer such as the lack of or use of tuning forks.

V.   There is a lack of documentation as to the reliability and accuracy of the speed detection device, police cruiser speedometer calibration or maintenance.

VI. You should also ask for a dismissal if the officer has not allowed you to look at the evidence against you at the scene of the traffic stop, namely, the speed detection device he was operating at the time of the stop.

Making a motion to dismiss may work before a judge or court official who is sincerely open minded, and willing to listen to some plausible theories about the case, and why the ticket should be thrown out. Such a motion may or may not work, but, it is certainly worth a try if you feel a situation exists that would warrant such a motion.

FINAL CASE SUMMATION

Once the state and defendant (you) have finished presenting their case before the court, you will be allowed to present a closing argument or final summation. The state and or arresting officer may have little to say. You, however, will now put all the pieces of your case together in such a way that it supports your defense theory and sheds doubt on the states case.

What you want to do here is present to the court, the strongest points of your case based on the testimony and physical evidence that was presented. You want to point out the weak parts of the states case also, along with any procedures that were not followed. Include statements like the arresting officer obtained a speed reading from another vehicle, and not yours; interference from some object in the area accounted for the speed reading obtained; no traffic history was taken by the officer; no tuning forks were used by the officer or the speed detection device was not properly calibrated or certified to be reliable and accurate; the patrol car's speedometer was not properly calibrated to be accurate and reliable; the officer was unqualified and not competent to be operating that speed detection device, and a wide array of others. Just be sure to try and tie in more than one of these statements to make your final argument a solid one.

Do not state that the arresting officer was wrong in any way. Use the word mistaken instead. Inform the court that you are an honest, law abiding citizen and believe you are innocent of the traffic violation that you are charged with. Be sincere, polite and confident. The court will recognize this and it may work in your favor. End your final summary with a statement to the court in which you feel the state has not presented or proven their case beyond a reasonable doubt, that you were not speeding and that you respectfully request a verdict of "not guilty".

The state will get to make their final summary also. Their summation will simply go over the elements of the citation and will assert that they have proven their case before the court. If you tried to show the arresting officer was not qualified and competent enough to be operating that speed detection device, the state may elect to point that out under Honeycutt vs Kentucky, only a few hours of instruction normally is enough to qualify an operator of police radar. They may also point out that police speed detection devices are accurate and reliable measurements of speed detection.

If you feel the need to add to your final summation, request the court to grant you permission to do so and then add facts that dispute the states case. Target those area which include the following. Since the Honeycutt, the NHTSA and the International Chief's of Police both recommend 24 hours of classroom instruction an 16 hours of supervised field experience for members of law enforcement to be adequately trained, and that the National Bureau of Standards has performed studies that show police radar did not meet standards deemed acceptable to them. Police traffic radar is full of false speed readings for a variety of different reasons and therefore, was held to be unreliable and inaccurate.

THE VERDICT

The judge will issue his verdict upon completion of the case by both the state and defense. It will be guilty or not guilty. I hope you have won and been found not guilty. If you did win, great and good job! If you didn't win, don't feel too bad, you gave it your best and at least you fought back. Not every person will win in court but the odds are great that you will win in some manner. You may have your fine reduced or the charge changed to something less than what you were originally charged with, so this should be considered a win anyway. Remember, you fought back, you did not just decide to pay the ticket and do nothing about it. That alone is a tremendous victory for you and your feeling of self worth. Additionally, you are now better prepared should you get stopped for speeding again. It is sad to say that there are some magistrates, prosecutors and judges who are so deeply implanted in this speeding ticket racket, that even with a good, solid defense, complete with loopholes, they may find a person guilty and this is unfortunate.

Many people still feel the need to fight a guilty verdict by appealing the courts decision. Be aware, this can be very expensive but if you feel you have a strong case, maybe an appeal is in order. Only you can decide if you want to appeal your conviction to the Appellate court in your state. And you may want to consider retaining the services of a competent attorney to assist you in that appeal. Good luck!

OTHER HELPFUL INFORMATION

Some other information that may enable you to beat a speeding ticket in court, include some of the following information.

Ⓥ A common practice for members of law enforcement is to try and make you think they are giving you a break or doing you a favor. They do this by stating to you at the scene of the traffic stop, that they are lowering the speed they claimed you were traveling at. What the officer will do is state that you were traveling at one speed, based on his speed detection device, but, then states he is lowering the speed to something else. For example, the officer indicates you were traveling 70 mph in a 55 mph zone, but elects to charge you with operating 65 mph in a 55 mph zone. If you have that mini cassette recorder, this conversation will be recorded and could be very useful later in court when you plead not guilty and ask for a hearing.

Why would the officer elect to do such a thing you may ask? Well, for a couple of reasons. The officer feels by lowering the speed he claims you were traveling at, the violator is more likely to pay the fine instead of pleading not guilty and going to court. Remember, members of law enforcement generally do not want to go to court for traffic offense cases. It is very time consuming for them. The other reason an officer may elect to do something like this, is because he was unable to accurately pick the target vehicle that was speeding as based on the speed detection unit being used. The officer stops your vehicle, and only guessed that it was in fact your vehicle traveling in excess of the speed limit. Due to his feeling a little unsure of himself, he elects to lower the amount of miles per hour you were exceeding the posted speed limit.

If this happens to you, you **MUST** plead not guilty. When you get to court, at the initial hearing, plead not guilty and tell the court official hearing the case what happened. State you have recorded the conversation and have it available for review if necessary. Point out the officer falsified or lied on the traffic ticket because they put down a speed that you were not actually traveling at. Be sure to maintain the fact that you were not speeding to begin with. This can really bring some doubt into this case, especially if a judge hears what the officer did in the issuance of a speeding ticket in that manner. It brings to mind what other things in that traffic stop did the officer "lie" about or fudge. Your chances of winning in a case like this could be very good.

Something similar to the tactic used by law enforcement as mentioned above, but not quite the same, is something called "radar estimated". This occurs when an officer is operating a speed detection device, and can not actually pick your vehicle out of a group of vehicles that are all traveling at about the same speed, at about the same time. A traffic stop will be made of a vehicle in that grouping, and the officer will issue a ticket based on his radar reading, and his estimation of your speed. The officer is almost admitting he is not sure of the actual speed of your vehicle.

In these types of tickets, again, plead not guilty. When you get to court, explain all of this to the court official. Estimated is just that, it is not actual. Then question the speed detection device used by the officer. Obtain the records from that law enforcement agency for the equipment, cruiser and officer and review it. In these types of cases, the ticket is usually dismissed or the fine lowered to a plea bargained out fine total. Always ask for a dismissal. If you are found responsible, ask for a trial by a judge and once there, explain the same thing as above. Use all of my tips, tactics and strategies for presenting a proper defense in court by yourself.

If you were issued a speeding ticket by a member of law enforcement, and you are very upset about it, this tip or tactic may interest you. Find out whom the officer was that cited you, when he works, and where. You will then follow that officer home from work in your own vehicle, and if possible, film or video tape this officer speeding as he heads home. Remember, he is a citizen and must follow all of the laws like everybody else. It is not right for him to issue tickets to people for something he himself does, and this includes speeding. If the officer observes you doing this, so what. He can not arrest you or stop you from exercising your constitutional right to prepare a case for trial.

Make notes about the speed or the officer, how long he was speeding for, how fast, where, the traffic conditions in the area, etc. You are trying to discredit the police officer in the eyes of the court. You may not beat your ticket by just doing this, but it certainly will help convince the clerk-magistrate, prosecutor or judge that this case should not go to trial to protect the officer from embarrassment. Further, it is very possible the officer may elect to not showing up at your trial out of fear of embarrassment. We know that if the officer does not show up in court, the case is usually dismissed and you have won!

A word to out of state residents who have found themselves stopped in another state for speeding. You may be taken before a clerk-magistrate or judge immediately for trial. Be prepared for that.

You could be fined and unless you are able to pay the fine, you may be held in county lockup until the money is available to pay and bail you out.

Additionally, if you receive a speeding ticket and are released with a court date of some sort, and you do not want to return to that state for trial, either send in a not guilty plea, or contact the courts district attorneys or prosecutors office and explain the situation to them. They may be very reasonable with you and just dismiss the ticket if you tell them you will never speed in their state again. You may also be given the option of sending your appeal in written form through the mail. It will be reviewed by the proper court official and you will be notified of the decision. Should this be an option, use all of the information I given you in this book to come up with a solid, convincible and factual defense. State you do not believe you were speeding. That there were other vehicles in the area and your vehicle was stopped in error. That there were objects in the area that produced spurious false speed readings, etc.

⑤ Some other points you should be aware of include, asking the clerk-magistrate, prosecutor or judge for a change in the actual charge. Many court officials will plea bargain with a person to avoid a trial and they may lower the fine or offer to change the offense from speeding to something quite different. For example, not wearing a safety belt. The courts want to prevent a trial and thus, reduce their caseload. This tactic works rather well I should add. So don't be afraid to try it for any traffic ticket you receive.

⑥ You should also know that the police officer himself, generally speaking, has the sole decision on what type of enforcement action he may give a traffic offender. It could be an oral warning, written warning, speeding infraction or a court appearance required citation. Don't be afraid to ask for a break of some kind from the officer.

⑦ There is one other method to beating a speeding ticket in court that I will mention briefly here, and that is having the ticket fixed in court by a friend who may be a cop himself, or by knowing somebody within the criminal justice system that could pull some strings for you. Do not believe that once a ticket has been issued, that there is nothing that can be done for you if you are trying to get it fixed. There are a lot of tickets fixed behind the scenes in courts all over the country. If you know somebody, this may be an alternative method to getting the ticket taken care of without having to go to trial yourself.

A couple of additional tips. One very important step in preparing for trial, that everybody must do upon receiving a speeding ticket is to review their own state laws as they pertain to speeding and or the violation that you were charged with. Many states list in their laws exactly what must take place in order for the courts to convict you, or specify how or when speed detection equipment must be calibrated or inspected. Many state laws also refer to case law or summaries which you should also review, just as any good lawyer would do prior to trial, to see what precedents have been set in any other case's which may help your case in court. Do not overlook doing this.

Additionally, when requesting records from the arresting police dept. you should send a letter to them, keeping a copy, certified mail with a return receipt request which will show proof of your letter being received by them. This is your attempt to make a "discovery" request for the records that may help you in court. Do not be surprised if you do not receive these records, them are seldom provided until the trial date, and some will even fail to have them on the day of the trial. In this case, let the court know, by showing them a copy of your letter and return receipt, and state that (based on most state laws) you have the right to examine the records that you requested, such as calibration records, and you are requesting they be provided for you so that you can prepare a defense in your behalf. You also may make a motion to dismiss if the records are not provided also.

"O.K. Folks... You're all guilty of going at least 65 mph in a 55 mph zone, stay to the right and form one line."

One tactic which law enforcement uses at the end of the month to fill their quota.

CHAPTER FOUR

LEARN TO SPEED AND NOT GET CAUGHT!

In this chapter, you will learn about the many tips, tactics and strategies that will enable you to speed more safely and effectively, without being detected or caught by the police.

Today's motorists have the choice of driving the speed limit or exceeding it. It is also true that today's modern, well built automobiles certainly do make speeding easy and convenient. People can learn certain tactics and strategies, and put them into practice that will minimize their risk of being singled out from the majority of traffic exceeding the speed limit. That is exactly what I will teach you about in this chapter, and who better to teach you but a former police officer. Due to my own experiences as a police officer, I have gained valuable knowledge on the many tips, tactics and strategies as they pertain to the subject of speeding, and I now share many of them with you.

It is important for me to first tell you that I am not advocating that anybody exceed the speed limit. I am simply informing the many people who choose to do so, how to do it safely and effectively, without getting detected or caught by the police. Yes, speed does, in many instances, increase the risk of accidents and or the loss of human life. Speed can be a contributing factor should something go wrong when a person is exceeding the speed limit or driving in a reckless manner.

What I do advocate is that everybody drive safe and reasonable upon the highways. Those who drive at high speeds, or in a reckless manner should expect to be stopped by members of law enforcement, and issued traffic tickets. These high-risk drivers are the ones who generally cause automobile accidents which claim the lives of innocent people. I am certainly against that kind of reckless driving.

As was already discussed throughout this book, there are many factors, most of them having nothing to do with highway safety, that might explain why you may be stopped and cited for speeding. Remember, at one time, these speeds of say, 65 mph were considered prudent and safe, and in fact should be. It could be a city, town or state that is trying to raise revenue through the issuance of speeding tickets. Or it could be that your state needs to show compliance through enforcement with the states set speed limits. Whatever the reason, the majority of speeding tickets that are issued are for speeds, that, in many states are considered legal, safe and reasonable, but are illegal and ticket issuable in others, even if the roadway and the driving conditions are the same!

Ironically, most speeding tickets are given for speeds that are neither extremely high or dangerously low. Most are given to people who are operating only slightly over the posted speed limit, by between 10 and 15 mph where the speed limit is set at 55 mph. The National Highway Traffic Safety Administration Act states the safest speeds to travel at or between 10-15 mph over because fewer accidents occur.

We can all blame the federal government for many of the speeding tickets being issued today in areas where the speed limit is or remains 55 mph. It was them in 1974 that passed the National Highway Safety Act, which made the nationwide speed limit 55 mph. At that time, the real emphasis on making the speed limit 55 mph nationwide was to conserve energy because of the oil crisis that existed at that time. Today, we really do not have an oil crisis since gasoline is plentiful and widely available.

It has only been in the past couple of years that many states have raised their own states speeding limits from 55 mph to speeds generally around 65 mph (although some states do have higher speeds on some of their highways). Many states have begun to raise their speeding limits because the federal government passed legislation allowing each state to set their own speed limits without the fear of losing federal moneys for interstate highway repair and maintenance.

There are many roads across the country that can very easily handle traffic traveling at speeds around 65 mph. Our roadways and highways are safer, wider and better constructed. Most people according to federal government studies, travel at speeds they consider safe and reasonable, and tend to ignore the posted speed limits that many experts feel are too low. Despite fears, people are not driving like nuts in areas where the speed limit was raised from 55 mph to 65 mph or higher. The publishers and myself realize that we are offering tips, tactics and strategies that tell a person how to break the law. Again, we feel that traveling at speeds considered safe and reasonable, even though they may exceed the legal posted speed limit in a particular state, is something that should be left up to each motorist. Today's automobiles and highways are safer and allow for speeds in excess of 55 mph. We feel the public has the right to be informed on how one can speed and reduce their chances of getting caught by the police.

Due to the revenue speeding tickets generate for both a state and the insurance industry, many states, Connecticut being one of them, have refused to raise their speed limits from the national speed limit of 55 mph. The sole motive in these states is the revenue, period, not highway safety. Once more, speeds that are considered safe, reasonable and legal in many sates, are illegal in other states, and members of the law enforcement community will stop, and ticket motorists who exceed the speed limit.

In a recent newspaper article both the American Automobile Association and the National Highway Traffic Safety Administration caution that it is too soon to draw any conclusions from the raising of the speed limit in many states. Since the federal government let states raise the limits last year, at least 10 have done so. Some states, the highway fatality rate was higher than the year before, but, in other states, the fatality rate fell. Many states are still gathering their data since their speed limits were raised. So the information is very preliminary at this point. But, it seems to be remaining somewhat consistent when averaged out across the country. Many people continue to drive safe and reasonable and appear to drive with the general flow of traffic the article seemed to indicate.

I hope you can now see why I have provided this information here to you in this chapter. Much of this material is directed toward the average citizen who may exceed the speed limit by 10 to 15 mph, yet is still driving safe and reasonable in a 55 mph speeding zone. In areas where the posted speed limit is 65 mph, operating anything more than 5 mph over that, I could consider to be somewhat unsafe and do not advocate that. A speed of 70 mph I feel is quite sufficient for travel on larger roadways and interstate highways and see no need to exceed it. On country, main and back roads, speeds of 45 to 55 mph would be the limit I would suggest a person travel, and for obvious reasons.

The publishers and myself realize that we are offering tips, tactics and strategies that tell a person how to break the law. Again, we feel that traveling at speeds considered safe and reasonable, even though they may exceed the legal posted speed limit in a particular state, is something that should be left up to each motorist. Todays automobiles and highways are safer and allow for speeds in excess of 55 mph. We feel the public has the right to be informed on how one can speed and reduce their chances of getting caught by the police.

Before I get into the actual tips on how one can speed without getting caught, I need to discuss one additional subject that many people seem to have a lot of questions about, and that is police quotas. Many people believe that the police have quotas that they must meet every month, and that is why increased enforcement is observed at the end of the month. Generally speaking, the police having a quota to meet every month, would be unethical if not illegal in most states. In the state of Connecticut for example, it is actually illegal for a law enforcement agency to have a quota system in place. What the Connecticut law allows, is that the data on the amount of traffic tickets issued, can be used in the evaluation of the employees work performance. All this, provided that the data is not the exclusive means to evaluate the performance of that employee. What exists as far as the number of tickets given by any one particular member of law enforcement, is something most employers have, and that is job performance and evaluation.

You see, when an officer comes onto any department or agency, their performance is evaluated on a regular basis. If that officer has consistently issued say, 50 tickets a month for the past year, he is expected to issue at least that many during the following evaluation period. If he does not, and issues less, his overall performance and evaluation will reflect that. Most law enforcement officers wish to get promoted, so many do not want a less than favorable evaluation in their work records. It is fair to say that at the end of the month or evaluation period, many officers feel forced to issue more tickets to receive that favorable evaluation. It can not however, be considered an actual quota.

LEARNING TO SPEED

Like any other skill, speeding is something that one must learn and practice in order to become effective, and good at it. In other words, a person must learn to sharpen their speeding skills if they wish to be successful. By following some of the many tips that will follow, one can expect to become a safer and more efficient speeder, and thus, will greatly reduce their chances of being detected and ticketed by a member of law enforcement.

Probably the most important tip that I could give you, is that you need to **PAY ATTENTION AT ALL TIMES!** Always drive in a manner where you are in control, and always are fully aware of what is in your environment or general area, and this includes police cruisers. You have mirrors and windows and of course, eyes, learn to use them constantly. Many people have been stopped by the police for speeding because they did not see the unmarked vehicle parked on the side of the road. You need to be alert for anything! You need to spot that police officer and his cruiser before he spots you. Yes, it can be tiring always being on the watch, but if you avoid getting stopped because you detected the presence of the police nearby, and adjusted your speed, you will have saved yourself from getting stopped and ticketed.

To learn to drive fast, you must also learn to vary your speed when conditions permit. For example, travel fast when it is safe to do so, and be prepared to drive slower when its sensible based on the time of day, the traffic flow, weather conditions and other factors.

Many of the following tips, tactics and strategies are useful only at certain times and under the right conditions. For example, some are only effective during the daytime, when one can see a cruiser parked on the side of the roadway. Others are useful at any time, like observing the brake lights come on in a vehicle traveling in front of your vehicle. You need to decide when and where each is most useful to you. You must also determine which is applicable to your driving habits.

THE TIPS, TACTICS AND STRATEGIES

1. <u>Pay attention and remain alert at all times</u>. Be on the watch for police cruisers in the area. Know what other vehicles are around you and your car at all times. Remaining alert and on guard is one of the most important tips I can tell you about.

2. <u>Use a radar/laser detector</u>. I know you did not buy this book to learn that the use of radar/laser detector is good advice, but it is!!! Coupled with my tips, tactics and strategies, the use of a quality detector will greatly reduce your chances of getting stopped for speeding and issued a ticket by a member of law enforcement.

3. <u>Always have a police monitor or scanner in your vehicle so that you can monitor the police band</u>. There are many books available on the market that tell you every law enforcement agencies frequency. Obtain the frequency, enter it into the scanner and listen to that band when traveling in that area. If you travel a lot and are in different states, obtain the police frequencies for each state and monitor the police activity as you enter the state. It is also helpful to learn the police codes that indicate what a traffic stop is or when an officer is in the process of requesting either license driver or registration history from the dispatcher. The closer and clearer the officer sounds on the scanner, the closer he is in the area, so slow down and be on the watch. Many times, the officer will tell dispatch his location anyway, for safety of the officer.

4. <u>Also, the use of or monitoring of a Citizen Band (CB) radio may also be helpful in the alerting of you to a potential police radar trap ahead or in the area</u>. Truckers are known for relaying to other motorists and truckers the locations of a speed trap when they observe one.

5. Police love to hide around the bend in the roadway, and then jump out to catch the target or speeding vehicle. To avoid

being detected or stopped, <u>be on the watch for the brake lights</u> <u>to come on from vehicles traveling in front of you</u>. If you observe this, slow down, there is usually a reason why that vehicle is braking. It could very well be a police officer hiding around the corner! <u>Learn to slow on all blind corners</u>!

6. <u>If you should spot or observe a police cruiser on the side of</u> <u>the road, as you round a corner or go over a hill, immediately</u> <u>hit the brakes and slow down</u>! Why? because the officer has to react to observing your speed on the speed detection device he is operating, and then he has to lock that speed in on the device. That takes time, and if you brake sharply but safely, you will greatly lower the speed at which he locks you in at. Hopefully, you have slowed so much that the officer decides not to stop you. This also shows the officer you are aware of your speed and are slowing down. Some motorists continue to speed right by a police cruiser, which, from my own experience, really gets the officer mad, and may make him more apt to go after, and stop that vehicle. If you do get stopped, make sure you ask to see your speed on the speed detection device the officer is using. If he refuses to allow this, be sure that the court official hearing your ticket appeal knows this. One other thing you should know is that if you are traveling around that corner or over that hill with other traffic, the officer may not know which vehicle is registering a certain speed according to the speed detection device being used. The officer may have to pick or choose the vehicle he thinks is speeding. Be sure to let this fact be known in court also if applicable.

7. <u>If you observe another vehicle getting stopped for speeding,</u> <u>don't assume that you are automatically safe to go speeding</u> <u>by that officer</u>. He can easily reset his speed detection device and go after you. Or he could be working in a team with another officer, who is waiting ahead to stop you once the description of your vehicle has been radioed to him. If you were issued a ticket in which two different officers were involved in the stop itself, be sure both get subpoenaed to

court to testify in the case. One or both of them may not show up.

8. <u>As a general rule, and depending on the highway, try not to speed in the right hand lane of a roadway.</u> Always try and speed in the high speed or left lane. There are some multiple lane highways, like the Mass. Pike in Massachusetts, where most of the police radar operated there is on the right hand side of the roadway. Generally, most motorists stopped for speeding are in the right or middle lanes. The motorist in the far left lane is usually not stopped due to the moderate to heavy traffic volume and the general high rate of speed the traffic is moving. On other roads, the police may be sitting on either side operating a speed detection device. A good rule to follow is speed in the left lane but travel in either the middle or right lane. Be on the watch for cruisers anywhere.

9. <u>Learn to speed in moderate to heavy traffic flows upon a high way.</u> The police do not like to operate speed detection devices in heavy traffic. It is not safe to do so and it is very difficult to stop a vehicle under these conditions. As I have mentioned earlier, the police enforce speeding limits when the conditions are the safest. Just be sure to drive safely and not recklessly. Traffic generally is flowing at speeds that are above the posted speed limit anyway.

10. <u>Be careful and try to avoid speeding down a hill or down a grade.</u> Some members of law enforcement like to catch speeders who do not control their speed coming down a hill. As we know, cars do increase speed as they go down any hill or incline, so keep your speed under control.

11. <u>The police also like to use highway on and off ramps to sit and operate a speed detection device.</u> Be cautious of this. Keep your eyes on the road, watch for the brake lights of other vehicles, and watch for cruisers parked on the ramps.

12. <u>Many members of law enforcement also like to sit on bridge over passes and operate radar or laser. Watch the bridge as you approach</u>. Is there a cruiser sitting up there operating some speed detection device, and does he have it point ed directly at you?

13. <u>Get in the habit of always watching your mirrors, both the side and rear view</u>. Watch for cruisers coming up from behind. If you are speeding, the cruiser could be "pacing" or "clocking" you. Many motorists get stopped this way because they did not see the cruiser behind them, until it was too late.

14. <u>Keep your eyes on interstate or major highways that have a crossable center roadway or drive</u>. Many police officers will often just sit there waiting for a car to go speeding by.

15. <u>Use extreme caution when entering a hospital or school zone because the speed usually drops to around 25 mph</u>. The police love to run radar in these areas, so be on the watch for it. Little tolerance is allowed in these areas also. I used to run a lot of radar in school zones because people really did drive excessively fast in these areas. A school zone is not an area where one should be exceeding the speed limit.

16. <u>You should also be careful to avoid speeding right in front of the police station</u>. This is something that really gets the police officer upset, seeing a motorist speed right by their station. Try to avoid it. Police do operate speed detection devices close by their departments.

17. <u>**Never** speed across a town, city or state line</u>. This is some thing that really upsets members of law enforcement too. Many law enforcement agencies operate speed detection and traffic enforcement right on their jurisdictions border, be it a town, a city or a state. The police do exist here and do this as a kind of a welcome wagon to their jurisdiction and speeding is not allowed. This is one tip that I would recommend every

body remember anytime they are about to cross a town, city or state line.

18. <u>Learn to take advantage of "rabbits," or a faster motorist that goes speeding by, and then tail or follow him.</u> Stay at least a quarter mile back and maintain a clear line of visibility at all times. If anybody will get stopped by a member of law enforcement operating a speed detection device ahead, it will be that speeding motorist you are following.

19. <u>You should also learn to recognize the front and rear lights of a police cruiser.</u> With practice, one will be able to recognize a cruiser in front or coming up from the rear at night, and take appropriate action by slowing down.

20. <u>ALWAYS slow down upon seeing ANY vehicle parked on the side of any roadway or highway.</u> The police use many different kinds of under cover vehicles to operate speed detection devices, including sports cars, vans and tractor trailer units. Be on the watch for this. Only increase your speed once you pass by that parked vehicle and feel that it is not occupied by a law enforcement officer.

21. <u>Learn to travel with the flow of traffic, even if the flow is exceeding the speed limit.</u> This makes detection by the police very difficult and will usually force them to pick the vehicle out of that group they feel was speeding.

22. <u>Speed in the left or passing lane as you go by a tractor trailer unit on the highway.</u> The truck will act as a shield for you to avoid being picked up by any speed detection device being operated in the area.

23. **<u>SLOW DOWN</u>** <u>in areas where you know the police usually run radar or some other speed detection device.</u> In other words, if you know where the speed traps are located, lower your speed as you approach that area.

24. <u>Learn to speed safely and avoid being detected by the police</u>. Do not drive recklessly or fail to use your turn signals and avoid sudden lane changes. This type of driving is targeted by the police with or without speed detection equipment in use. Speeding safely reduces your risks of an accident, and in getting stopped. Remember, almost everybody has a cellular phone now, and somebody could call the police with your vehicle description and plate number and report your driving habits. Nobody wants the police looking for them!

25. <u>Learn to drive only 10 to 15 mph over the posted speed limit</u>. By doing this, you will reduce your chances of getting stopped and issued a speeding ticket. The police in most areas do generally allow a motorist to exceed the posted speed limit about 10 to 15 mph on a multiple lane highway or interstate highway. Stick to this policy, and follow the general flow of traffic and you should be fine. If you speed excessively, you can expect your chances of getting stopped by the police to increase also.

26. <u>Do not be fooled by observing one police cruiser parked on the side of the roadway. There could be one or more just ahead.</u> The police do sometimes work in teams, and people sometimes fccl safc after they pass by a cruiser running a speed detection device, and do not expect to see another cruiser doing the very same thing a half mile away.

27. <u>Watch for the motorist traveling in the opposite direction who is flashing their headlights in a series of rapid motions.</u> This is usually a good indicator that the motorist has observed a speed trap being operated by the police ahead, and in the direction that you are traveling.

28. <u>Weather conditions should dictate how fast you should be traveling</u>. As a general precaution, do not overdo it. The police usually do not operate speed detection devices or set up speed traps in poor weather, be it rain, snow or fog. Speed detection devices are less effective in bad weather, and members of law enforcement do not want to get wet anyway!

29. <u>The type of roadway should also dictate how fast one should travel</u>. It is far easier, and safer to speed or just follow the general traffic flow on a roadway(such as a multiple lane or interstate highway) than it is to speed on a back road. Remember, you want to speed, but you want to do it in a safe manner and one that will not be bringing attention to yourself from the police.

30. <u>Learn to speed in spurts</u>. In other words, if you are speeding along in an area of the highway that allows for a clear view ahead for a certain length of distance, and you are able to observe that there are no cruisers or unmarked vehicles any where, feel free to speed, until you approach that hill or blind corner. There, slow down until it is safe and visible to increase your speed again. This will greatly reduce your chances of being picked up on radar or another speed detection device and allows you to continue speeding in a safe and sure manner.

31. <u>In approaching a blind corner or hill, reduce your speed and fall in behind another vehicle.</u> This will prevent your vehicle from being the target of a speed detection device in the area. This vehicle you have pulled behind will act as a shield for you.

32. <u>If you live in a small town or city, know how your police department</u> operates. Learn how many police cruisers are out on patrol at any one time. Through the use of a police scanner, you should know where they are at all times. You see them parked at the police station or at some other place in town. You are now almost free to speed any place you want in town because you know where the police are at!

33. <u>Learn when shift changes occur in the law enforcement agencies in your area.</u> Is it a 7 to 3, 3 to 11 and a 11 to 7 shift change, or an 8 to 4, 4 to 12 and a 12 to 8 cycle? This is important to know because about 15 to 30 minutes before the shift change and about 15 to 30 minutes after the shift change,

there is usually no police presence on the streets. The police are not running radar at these times. Be careful for that speeding cop going to or from work, he may stop you if you are driving too fast. They also might be getting gas for the cruisers and are headed into the station to complete their end of shift duties or they are in roll call or just talking to other department members and will not usually hit the road until well after the beginning of their shift. This, therefore, is a good time to consider speeding through a given town, city or state.

34. <u>Avoid excessive speeding on sparsely traveled highways</u>. There will be no cover for you against radar. This applies both day and night.

35. <u>Drive a low-profile car.</u> Red Corvettes and Mustangs do get stopped before Escorts and Metros. Also, care for your car. Keep it clean and be sure all you lights work too.

If the unfortunate does happen, and you do get stopped for a speeding violation, make sure the excuse you give to that law enforcement officer is a good one. Some excuses or explanations are better than others, and a good one may even get you out of a ticket.

Above all, be polite, courteous and cooperative with the law enforcement officer whom stops you. The police are people too and have feelings. The worse thing that one can do is to upset an officer. You will surely get a ticket if you do that. I know this from my own experiences as a law enforcement officer. If you are nice, polite and have a good explanation, you may get a break. Do not be afraid to ask the officer for a break or a warning. Be sure you say please, look him in the eyes too. Use that excuse or explanation. Some of the better ones that I found myself falling for, were the ones that touched the heart. Like the following:

a. The money to pay the ticket will come from the same money that is used to feed, clothe and shelter the kids.

b. The wife is pregnant and money is very tight.

c. The person is in college, studying criminal justice and a speeding ticket could ruin all chances of getting a job in the law enforcement field.

d. The sick relative or death in family excuse also works very well.

e. Inform the officer you were just coming from your doctors office and you found out today that you have been diagnosed with cancer and to receive a speeding ticket would only make their life more miserable.

f. Tell the officer you need to get to a restroom badly and quickly because of kidney or bowel problems.

g. Indicate to the officer (if true) that you don't understand or speak English very well. He may get frustrated and let you go.

Whatever excuse or explanation you use, be sure it is genuine, real and sincere. Do not use the late for work or not paying attention excuse. They don't work very well because in the eyes of the officer, you should have been more attentive to the time and or the speed at which you were traveling.

That just about concludes this chapter. I hope you can use some of this information to your benefit. Remember, becoming a good speeder takes time, effort and practice. By using some of these tips, tactics and strategies, one can expect to accomplish just that. Please, speed or exceed the speed limit in a safe and reasonable manner. Traveling at high rates of speed does not get you any place any faster. It could even get you a speeding ticket or cost you or others, their life, so please drive sensible.

EPILOGUE

A FINAL WORD FROM THE AUTHOR

I hope that you have used my tips, tactics and strategies to become a safer and more efficient speeder or you have been successful in fighting a speeding ticket in court. I know that by reading the material contained in this book, you now have more knowledge about the subject of speeding than most people in today's society, including the police and even lawyers.

Your knowledge will better protect you from getting caught in a police speed trap. You will be better able to beat that ticket right there at the scene of the traffic stop by questioning the law enforcement officer as we have outlined. You are also now better prepared to fight a speeding ticket in a court of law than a lawyer is.

People like you and me can make a difference in the long run if more and more people challenge the system . The system whose sole intent is the revenue it earns from the issuing of speeding tickets. We have the power to change the attitude of the many people whom just feel they should pay the fine and mail it in. Tell people about this book, and the others out there like it. Pass it around and let them read it. If you know somebody who got a speeding ticket, tell them that they should fight it in court and show them how! Much of the information contained in my book is applicable in all 50 states too.

I sincerely hope that anyone who has taken the time to read my book, found it to be an excellent source of information. The book took a lot of work, time and patience because I wanted to do it right. I wanted a book that everybody could read and understand. I hope that I have accomplished just that.

If you find yourself heading to traffic court because of a speeding ticket, and you need the studies about radar, laser and VASCAR's weaknesses, or you have any questions, call us toll free at 1-888-344-4836 and we will try to help you out in any way we can.

I would love to hear from you with your suggestions, stories, comments or criticisms. Thank you and God Bless!

APPENDIX "A"
IMPORTANT CASE LAW CITING
INVOLVING POLICE RADAR

Some of the more important court decisions that have all come down over the years that involve the use and application of police radar, are included here in the Appendix for your information. These court excerpts should only be used as a general guide for your information. One should consult a law library in their respective state to obtain further information about each of these cases. Doing a little research in this area may prove to be very beneficial to an individual who intends to represent himself in a court of law. These court cases will most likely present that person with solid defense strategies and may even result in that person winning their case in court.

STATE OF FLORIDA (DADE CTY) VS. AQUILERA (1979)

This famous case, which took place in Florida, was also known as the Miami Trial because of all the publicity that the case received. At issue here was the reliability of police radar. The public learned that there were no standards for police radar and no police training. The judge on the case, the Honorable Nesbitt, dismissed a speeding ticket issued to Anna Aquilera, citing that police radar had not been proven reliable and accurate in every situation beyond any reasonable doubt. The judge went on to further state that the traffic court is there not only to convict, but to acquit the innocent, and not to be a revenue collection agency for the state or county.

Arising out of this case, the federal government began to test various police radar units, along with agencies it contracted to perform additional testing. Its own studies revealed many flaws with the police radar, including but not limited to electromagnetic interference, shadowing, batching, panning error, scanning error, cosine angular effect, internal and external interference which all produced false speeding readings.

STATE OF FLORIDA VS ALLWEISS, (1980)

A Pinellas County Court in this case, ruled that the testing procedures for all police radar had to include the use of a tuning fork to calibrate or self test the unit. And that tuning fork had to be used by law enforcement in calibrating the radar units when used in traffic stops. Allweiss was found not guilty in this case.

STATE OF NEW JERSEY VS DANTONIO, (1955)

The Supreme Court of New Jersey, in this decision ruled that police radar itself was only one piece of evidence in the entire case when the state attempted to convict a person for a speeding violation. They further stated that NO expert testimony was necessary provided that the police using the radar set it up and calibrated it properly. They said the speed readings given from the radar unit were admissible as evidence to be weighed with other evidence given, and errors with the police radar would only affect the weight it carries as evidence itself. Dantonio was found guilty in this case.

STATE OF DELAWARE VS. EDWARDS, (1980)

The court of Commons Pleas in Delaware found Edwards not guilty because the court felt the evidence given from the radar unit being used, was not sufficient to be the sole reason for a conviction. The court felt that the radar unit had not been proven reliable or trustworthy.

THE UNITED STATES VS. FIELDS, (1982 Ohio)

The District Court in this case held that it was impossible to know if the police radar unit was measuring the speed of Fields or from some other object. Further, the court felt the operator of the unit was not properly qualified. Nor did he calibrate the unit by the use of a tuning fork. Therefore, the court found Fields not guilty. The court questioned the reliability of police radar based on areas of interference that exist in its beam range.

THE STATE OF MINNESOTA VS. GERDES (1971)

The Supreme Court of Minnesota ruled in this case, that expert testimony is not necessary in cases where police radar is used. However, there needs to be a way to provide the accuracy and the reliability of a particular device, and set forth guidelines for that state. They include proper training and experience for the officer operating the unit; the officer has to testify how the unit was set up; that the unit was operating in an area where there was minimum distortion, interference or spurious readings and that a tuning fork must be used to confirm the accuracy and reliability of the unit in use at the time of the stop. Gerdes' original conviction from a lower court was reversed.

THE STATE OF WISCONSIN VS. HANSON, (1978)

The Wisconsin Supreme Court in this case set minimum standards for the use of police radar as evidence. Courts in that state can not take accuracy and reliability of police radar to be prima facie, or that it stands on its own as being both reliable and accurate. Those guidelines included proper training for the officer, that the the unit must have been working properly at the time of the arrest, there was minimal interference in the general area, and the unit was tested by means other than its own internal calibration. Hanson had his conviction from the lower court reversed and remanded.

COMMONWEALTH OF KENTUCKY VS. HONEYCUTT (1966)

The Kentucky Court of Appeals in this case affirmed the conviction of Honeycutt, but set forth guidelines for that states use of police radar. The court said that a properly operated radar unit is capable of accurately measuring the speed of a motor vehicle. The court also stated that it will accept testimony that the unit was calibrated shortly before the stop was made, and that operator is not required to understand the scientific principles of radar, but does need to properly set up, test and operate such units. Normally a few hours of instruction is all that is necessary. It also required that the radar's target should be out in front, by itself and the vehicle that is nearest to the radar unit being operated.

STATE OF OHIO VS. OBERHAUS, (1983)

The Municipal Court in this state sustained a motion to suppress the results of a K-55 police radar unit that was used in the moving mode. The court stated stationary mode was the mode it would allow and accept in the state. Moving mode was, therefore, not allowed. Oberhaus was found not guilty.

STATE OF NEW YORK VS. PERLMAN, (1977)

The Suffolk County District Court found Perlman not guilty on a speeding ticket because it ruled that the radar device was not proven to be accurate or reliable because no external test had been done before or after the stop. Further, there was no record of testing on the unit at all.

STATE OF CONNECTICUT VS. TOMANELLI, (1966)

The Connecticut Supreme Court in 1966, ruled that tuning forks must be used before and after each motor vehicle stop to show that the unit was accurate and reliable. Further, that tuning forks in the speeds of 40, 60, and 80 mph were used to indicate the unit was working properly. The court also stated that no effort was made by a defendant to attack the accuracy of the tuning fork themselves.

There are different case summaries and histories to be found in every state. Most set down what is and what is not allowed in the area of speed detection devices. It is a good idea to do some research in your own state in this area prior to your going to court to fight your speeding ticket.

STATE	SPEED DETECTION DEVICES USED.	DEVICE ANNUAL CALIBRATION	STATES OVER 21 DWI LEVEL	UNDER 21 DWI LEVEL	STATES MAX SPEED LIMIT	CASE LAW & MISC. INFO.
ALABAMA	RADAR	NONE REQUIRED	0.08	0.08	70 ON INTERSTATE	P.O.'S Do Calibration
ALASKA	RADAR	YES	0.10	0.00	65 MPH	
ARIZONA	ALL TYPES	YES	0.10	0.02	65 MPH	
ARKANSAS	RADAR	YES	0.10	0.02	65 MPH	
CALIFORNIA	ALL TYPES	YES	0.08	0.01	70 MPH	
COLORADO	ALL TYPES	YES	0.10	0.02	65 MPH	EDWARDS, 1980
CONNECTICUT	ALL TYPES	YES, SEMI ANN.	0.10	0.02	65 MPH	TOMANELLI, 1966
DELAWARE	ALL TYPES	YES	0.10	0.02	65 MPH	EDWARDS-1980
DISTR. COLUMB. **	RADAR	YES	0.10	0.00	50MPH OR R&P	
FLORIDA	ALL TYPES	YES	0.08	0.08	65 MPH	ALLWEISS/AQUILERA
GEORGIA	ALL TYPES	YES	0.08	0.04	65 MPH	
HAWAII	ALL TYPES	YES	0.08	0.08	55 MPH	
IDAHO	ALL TYPES	YES	0.10	0.02	65 MPH	
ILLINOIS	RADAR/LASER	YES	0.10	0.00	65 MPH	
INDIANA	ALL TYPES	YES, YEARLY	0.10	0.10	65 MPH	
IOWA	RADAR/VASCAR	YES	0.10	0.02	65 MPH	
KANSAS	ALL TYPES	YES	0.08	0.08	75-DAY, 70-NIGHT	
KENTUCKY	ALL TYPES	YES	0.05-0.10	0.05-0.10	65 MPH	HONEYCUTT-1966
LOUISIANA	ALL TYPES	YES	0.10	0.04	65 MPH	
MAINE	ALL TYPES	YES	0.08	0.00	AS POSTED	
MARYLAND	ALL TYPES	YES	0.10	0.02	65 MPH	
MASSACHUSETTS	ALL TYPES	YES	0.08	0.02	65 MPH	LASER NEW
MICHIGAN	ALL TYPES	YES	0.07	0.02	65 MPH	
MINNESOTA	ALL TYPES	YES	0.10	0.10	65 MPH	GERDES-1971
MISSISSIPPI	RADAR/VASCAR	YES	0.10	0.08	65 MPH	
MISSOURI	ALL TYPES	YES	0.10	0.10	70-DAY, 65-NIGHT	
MONTANA	RADAR	YES	0.10	0.02	65 MPH/AS POSTED	
NEBRASKA	ALL TYPES	YES	0.10	0.02	65 MPH	
NEVADA	RADAR/VASCAR	YES	0.10	0.10	75 MPH	
NEW HAMPSHIRE	RADAR/VASCAR	YES	0.08	0.02	65 MPH	NO SEAT BELT LAW

STATE MOTOR VEHICLE INFORMATION CHART

STATE	SPEED DETECTION DEVICES USED	DEVICE ANNUAL CALIBRATION	STATES OVER 21 DWI LEVEL	UNDER 21 DWI LEVEL	STATES MAX. SPEED LIMIT	CASE LAW & MISC. INFO.
NEW JERSEY	ALL TYPES	YES	0.10	0.10	FIXED OR 55 MPH	DANTONIO-1955
NEW MEXICO	RADAR	YES	0.08	0.02	65 MPH	
NEW YORK	ALL TYPES	YES	0.10	0.10	65 MPH	PERLMAN-77, BECK-NY
NORTH CAROLINA	RADAR/LASER	YES	0.08	0.08	65 MPH	
NORTH DAKOTA	RADAR/AIRCRAFT	YES	0.10	0.10	65 MPH	
OHIO	ALL TYPES	YES	0.10	0.02(-18YRS)	65 MPH	SHELT/AKRON/FIELDS
OKLAHOMA	RADAR/VASCAR	YES	0.10	0.10	70 MPH	
OREGON	ALL TYPES	YES	0.08	0.08	65 MPH	
PENNSYLVANIA	RADAR/VASCAR	YES	0.10	0.04	65 MPH	
RHODE ISLAND	RADAR/LASER	YES	0.10	0.10	65 MPH	T.FORK-NOT REQUIRED
SOUTH CAROLINA	ALL TYPES	YES	0.05	0.05	65 MPH	
SOUTH DAKOTA	RADAR/AIRCRAFT	YES	0.10	0.00	70-DAY, 65-NIGHT	
TENNESSEE	ALL TYPES	YES	0.10	0.02	65 MPH	
TEXAS	ALL TYPES	YES	0.10	0.10	70 MPH	
UTAH	RADAR/AIRCRAFT	YES	0.08	0.08	REAS.&PRUDENT	
VERMONT	RADAR	YES	0.08	0.02	65 MPH	
VIRGINIA **	RADAR/VASCAR	YES	0.08	0.02	65 MPH	
WASHINGTON	RADAR/AIRCRAFT	YES	0.10	0.02	65 MPH	
WEST VIRGINIA	RADAR	YES	0.10	0.02	65 MPH	
WISCONSIN	ALL TYPES	YES	0.10	0.10	65 MPH OR R & P	HANSON-1978
WYOMING	RADAR	YES	0.10	0.10	75 MPH IN RURAL	

*ONLY THE STATE OF NEW HAMPSHIRE DOES NOT HAVE A MANDATORY FRONT SEAT DRIVER OR PASSENGER SEAT BELT LAW.

**RADAR DETECTORS ARE ILLEGAL IN THESE TWO STATES.

***ALL TYPES OF SPEED DETECION DEVICES CAN INCLUDE RADAR, VASCAR, LASER, AIRCRAFT, AND PACING OR CLOCKING.

****MANY STATES REQUIRE SOME TYPE OF SPEED DETECTION DEVICE INSPECTION OR CERTIFICATION ON A YEARLY OR SEMI-YEARLY BASIS. THIS INSPECTION INCLUDES ANY CALIBRATION DEVICES SUCH AS TUNING FORKS. MANY STATES ALSO REQUIRE THEIR OFFICERS RECEIVE SOME TYPE OF ANNUAL RE-TRAINING IN THE USE OF SPEED DETECTION DEVICES. ONE SHOULD CONSULT THEIR OWN STATES RECORDS AND SEE WHAT THE REQUIREMENTS ARE.

*****IN ALL 50 STATES, THE D.W.I./O.U.I. LEVEL FOR COMMERCIAL DRIVERS(TRUCKERS) IS 0.04 AS PER FEDERAL D.O.T. GUIDELINES.

OTHER RESOURCES

The following is a list of other resources and or publications that you may find useful or helpful. All of them have subject material similar to that contained in this book.

1. **FIGHT YOUR OWN TICKET** by David Brown
   Nolo Press, contact them at (415)549-1976

2. **HOW TO WIN IN TRAFFIC COURT** by Phil Bello
   Major Market Books, 146 S. Lakeview Dr. Suite 300, Gibbsboro, NJ 08026

3. **TRAFFIC COURT: HOW TO WIN** by James Glass
   Allanby Press, 701 First Ave., Suite 272, Arcadia, CA 91006

4. **A FORMER PROSECUTOR TELLS HOW TO WIN YOUR CASE IN TRAFFIC COURT** by Charles Rubin
   1888 Century Park East, L.A., CA 90067. (213) 879-0111

5. **THE TICKET BOOK** by Rod Dornsife
   PO Box 1087, La Jolla, CA 92038

6. **A SPEEDERS GUIDE TO AVOIDING TICKETS**
   by James Eagan, Avon Books

7. **BEATING THE RADAR RAP** by John Tomerlin
   Contact him at 800-448-5170

8. **HOW TO TALK YOUR WAY OUT OF A TRAFFIC TICKET** by David Kelly
   Mark III Productions, PO Box 586, Yuba City CA 05992

9. **101+ WAYS TO GET OUT OF A TRAFFIC TICKET** by Jeff Hodge.
   Talent World Prod., PO Box 711090, Houston TX 77271

10. **"BEAT THE COPS"** by Alex Caroll
    AceCo Publishers, 924 Chapala St., Suite D, Santa Barbara, CA 03101, 800-322-6946

LATE ADDITIONAL TIPS

The reason you are requesting to get a copy of the arresting dept's. FCC license, is because radar, like police radio's, operates on a frequency, and thus, radio waves and just like police radio's, a dept. has to have listed on their license their radar unit's frequencies to be legally licensed to operate them as per FCC guidelines. Many depts. do not have FCC license's for their radar equipment, so request a copy of that FCC license, it may be important.

In some states, courts are actually allowing speeding violators to make a donation in lieu of paying a fine, to some needy organization, such as D.A.R.E., so ask, this may be another option for you to follow.

An additional tip I must tell you, having learned from many people who have made this mistake, is never, never, never tell the court you are there because you are worried your insurance premiums are going to go up if you are convicted for a speeding ticket, and that is why you are there in court to fight your ticket. Your as good as dead in the water if you state this. The only thing the court is, or should be concerned with, is your guilt or innocense, in the case before them, not your insurance premiums.

INDEX

ORDER FORM

PHONE ORDERS CALL TOLL FREE AT:

1-888-FIGHT-EM
(1-888-344-4836)

MAIL ORDERS TO:

Dwight-Wallace Enterprises
Attention Customer Service
210 Park Avenue, Suite 234
Worcester, MA 01609

PLEASE SEND ME___COPIES OF BEAT AND AVOID!

NAME:_____
COMPANY NAME:_____
ADDRESS:_____
CITY:_____
STATE:_____**ZIP:**_____
PHONE #:_____

Price is $19.95 plus $3.95 Postage & Handling
Priority Mail: Please add $3.00
Overnight Mail: Please add $15.00
(Mass. Residents Please Add 5% sales tax)

PAYMENT METHODS *(Please circle one)*
CHECK   MONEY ORDER   VISA   MC

CREDIT CARD #   -   -   -
EXP. DATE:
SIGNATURE:
THANK YOU FOR YOUR ORDER!!!